MIND MANAGING

MIND MANAGING
Using Your Thoughts,
Feelings, and Behaviors
For Health and
Self-Development

ALEXANDER CHAPUNOFF

FOREL

MIND MANAGING
Using Your Thoughts, Feelings, and Behaviors For Health
and Self-Development
All Rights Reserved.
Copyright © 2008 Alexander Chapunoff

This book may not be reproduced, transmitted, or stored in whole or in
part by any means, including graphic, electronic, or mechanical, without
the express written consent of the publisher except in the case of brief
quotations embodied in critical articles and reviews.

Published by Forel Books

ISBN-13: 978-0615442358
ISBN-10: 0615442358

Printed in the United States of America

Contents

Chapter 1
MIND MANAGING IN CONTEXT   1

Chapter 2
THOUGHTS, FEELINGS, AND BEHAVIORS   10

Chapter 3
THE PERSONALITY   19

Chapter 4
CHOICE OF MIND   27

Chapter 5
KNOWING THE OBSTACLES   35

Chapter 6
UNDERSTANDING THE MENTAL OBSTACLES   43

Chapter 7
UNDERSTANDING THE EMOTIONAL OBSTACLES 57

Chapter 8
UNDERSTANDING THE BEHAVIORAL OBSTACLES 71

An Interlude of Issues 77

Chapter 9
RELATIONSHIPS 79

Chapter 10
ADDICTION 84

Chapter 11
NEUROSIS AND PSYCHOSIS 95

Chapter 12
LIFESTYLE 100

Chapter 13
PRACTICES 107

Chapter 14
CONCLUDING REMARKS 130

Suggested Reading 135

Because the sage always confronts difficulties, he never experiences them.

—Lao Tsu

Chapter 1
Mind Managing in Context

Psychology has many schools of thought and is rich and broad enough to be many things to many people. But it can basically be described as the science of thought, feeling, and behavior. We all know these three expressions of the mind from personal experience; their validity is beyond dispute. But what not everyone knows is the practical *understanding* and *control* of these three phenomena. Because society has adopted a corrective (as opposed to preventive) approach to mental health, the dynamics of psychological empowerment aren't a part of most people's formal education. Most of us aren't prepared to handle our minds. It's thus no surprise that distress and conflict are more common than they should be.

Perhaps you yourself are reading this book out of a desire to do better. Consider the following: Have your thoughts ever raced wildly, seemingly with a "mind of their own," and you felt powerless to stop them? Has someone ever said something insulting to you and you were so upset it ruined your whole day or even affected your self-esteem or made you think about getting even? Have you ever wondered why you keep engaging in the same unhealthy habits, year after year, and don't break them although you know you should?

If you answered "yes" to any of these questions, welcome to the human race. It's one of those mysteries of life that while thoughts, feelings, and behaviors are natural and effortless in themselves, their reasoned and purposeful management is nowhere near as automatic. If anything, it's quite challenging; possibly, a reason for this is that the needed techniques aren't instilled in us while we're very young—things learned in childhood seem the most natural and so are performed with greater ease. So it's left for us to grow up and figure it all out when we become maladjusted or unhappy; in a sense, this is as good a time as any since our motivation to feel better is likely quite high; on the other hand, it's the moment when we're most vulnerable.

The most worthwhile self-help or therapy methods are those whose effectiveness can be easily verified because they were developed from the type of experience and observation readily accessible to anyone, not from theories or intellectualized concepts. You can then assess for yourself whether or not they work. I've often been asked, "How can I tell if my counselor or psychologist is any good?" My response is always, "By the results they bring. Whether they help you find answers and feel better." That's all, really. You can generally judge the quality of something by the results it produces.

The purpose of psychology is to help you understand yourself better, function more freely, and to that extent improve your life. Your mind plays a key role in this process. And since everything you do in life is due to your mind, it's of basic value to learn how to work with it more skillfully. At heart, psychology is a practical field: learning how to manage your mind results in greater daily satisfaction and happiness. This sense of joy feels genuine because it's well-earned; it doesn't come from avoiding difficulties but from resolving them. (As we'll discuss later, true joy comes, in part, from being able to experience and handle sorrow or stress so that you can move through, or with, it.) Allowing for happiness of this sort is important. For what could be more useful than happiness? When you really get down to it, what's the point of anything if you're unhappy? As we've learned from following celebrities, coveted things such as fame and fortune or power and popularity are empty (or worse, heavy burdens) in the absence of well-earned joy and contentment.

In this book, mind managing is offered as a simple

system that emphasizes your pro-active understanding and control of the three mental phenomena: thoughts, feelings, and behaviors. The material is akin to Jnana yoga (the yoga of knowledge) in that it discusses what's going on with your mind, what some of your possibilities are, and how you can apply this information. Toward the end of the book (Chapter 13) there are specific practices to help you use the content. But any knowledge that induces you to change something in you—even if it's just your view—is a practice in itself. The key question is: Is it helpful to you?

Limits of the Conscious Mind

Before learning how to manage the conscious mind (usually referred to in this book as "the mind"), let's put it in perspective by noting its limitations—what it can and can't do. As we will soon see, these limitations are helpful to know because they indicate the difference between *reality* (what is) and *mentality* (what the mind thinks and perceives). We typically equate both phenomena; yet the mind only knows mentality.

The conscious mind has two principal operations: *sensing* (organizing the perceptions of the five senses) and *thinking* (translating ideas and sensory perceptions into language). Though they are useful and convenient activities that serve many practical purposes in daily living, both are subjective and undependable. Studies on eyewitness testimony, memory, and sense perception have shown that these phenomena have less validity and reliability than is commonly supposed. While helpful, they are not a sure support. Personal experience further shows us how misleading our recollections and impressions can be, and how they can often disagree with those of others.

With respect to sensing, quantum physics has demonstrated that each mind constructs its own sensory experience, as opposed to truthfully perceiving a universal objective reality; and while, to some extent, a consensus (shared) reality is developed by society, the consensus is hardly absolute—to a color-blind person, for instance, red lips and a green lawn are the same color.

Thinking has its particular limitations as well. Reason and logic are the highest functions of the thinking mind and yet totally depend on valid data in order to be of any real value; the less of this there is, the more fallible the resulting reason and logic. Take 14th century Europe, for example. In that culture, it was considered unreasonable to believe that if a man continued traveling in a straight line north from Paris, he would eventually arrive back in Paris from the south. The logical conclusion at the time was that the earth was flat because on a spherical earth things would "fall off," so the belief was judged deranged since it defied the available data as it was then understood. Even if a man had been observed leaving Paris in a northerly direction and returning years later from the south, he would have likely been accused of trickery, perhaps even black magic. It was only in the following centuries that Europeans acquired more data and realized the belief was completely accurate.

Similarly, to have visited the court of Henry VIII and uttered the statement, "Elvis Presley is the king of rock and roll," would have been considered incomprehensible and absurd to the point of madness, while today in our culture there is information—and a context—to support it. Again, quantum physics has shown how each mind molds reality (actually, mentality) through its knowledge base and expectations: change these and its "reality" changes with them.

The Will Beyond the Conscious Mind

Despite their limitations, sensing and thinking remain valuable skills. The conscious mind isn't really the problem so much as our assuming that its productions are equivalent to whole truth. This assumption is the root of many psychological conflicts; it can attach us strongly to our ideas and perceptions so that we take them too seriously and either get defensive over them or feel unwilling to let them go when it's time to grow. Or else we may be frightened and inhibited by them, feeling so sure of whatever "terrible truth" we discovered. We can spend a lot of time and energy struggling with ourselves, life, the world, and other people when really we're just struggling with our own mind. We get misled by the pressure to conform to how right we are, even though it's keeping us unhappy. We keep charging at windmills because we haven't identified the root of the conflict: we haven't emotionally discovered that what our mind thinks and perceives is—at most—a partial (relative) truth and not the whole truth.

A corollary to this is how we equate the everyday personal self (the self our mind perceives and thinks about) with our total identity. We, in effect, ignore the whole aspect of the self in order to pursue the partial, often to the extent that we aren't even aware we have a "whole aspect" of self.

At some point after you start observing and analyzing your mind more closely, you might experience this issue of the whole self. The question may occur to you: If I'm *managing* my mind then how could I *be* my mind? If I'm working with my mind and all its thoughts, feelings, and behaviors then I must be something more. My intelligence and mind can't be synonymous. There must be something about my consciousness which is bigger than my mind.

A good analogy is your eyes. Whatever your eyes see can not be your eyes themselves because they're looking out through that very place. Your eyes have never, and will never, see themselves. They may see "themselves" in a mirror or reflection or photograph but those are just images *of* your eyes, not your real eyes. Similarly, whatever you think, or sense, about you can't be you since you yourself can't perceive you. When you think about your *identity* or perceive your *body,* these are *of* you. But not you yourself.

So who or what is this "you" that is behind your mind and body? This question brings us to the subject of the *will* (a psychological term) or *spirit* (a religious term). In either case, it refers to the subtle original consciousness expressed more outwardly by your mind and body. (For an interesting perspective on the will, see the psychosynthesis work of Roberto Assagioli.)

While this book doesn't deal explicitly with the will, I think it's helpful to acknowledge it here for the purpose of being holistic and to place mind managing in its natural context. Including the will as a reference point can help us get better oriented, with some perspective of the "big picture."

You might ask, "I know where my body is. But where is my will?" It is here, where you are. A better question might be, "When is my will?" It is now. Or maybe just before its personality vehicle (what you normally think of as you) thinks.

The will is your state of greatest energy and harmony; the part of you that cooperates with the universe and its laws (whether known by your mind or not), helping fulfill your place and function therein. It has sympathy with the universe. But at some point it was likely distracted by ongoing phenomena such as thinking, culture, habit, desire, conditioning, and so on. This distracted part of the will is what we usually term our *personality*. Normally, this personal self (or ego) is given much importance and the universal self (or will) isn't even noticed; mind managing addresses this imbalance—rather indirectly—by stimulating the aspect of the conscious mind that is *active* and nearer to the will and emphasizing it over the aspect that is *passive-reactive* and nearer to the ego (the issue will be discussed in more detail beginning in Chapter 4). So though direct awareness of the will is, strictly speaking, not necessary to achieve emotional health, knowledge of it as a concept can serve as a guide or beacon that shapes your understanding and directs your progress.

In a nutshell, this book proposes to increase your familiarity with how your conscious mind works in order to help you embark on a journey of self-awareness and discovery. In a sense, you are both passenger and conductor . . . so welcome aboard!

Chapter 2
Thoughts, Feelings, and Behaviors

Let's begin by discussing the three mental components—thoughts, feelings, and behaviors—and defining them precisely. Defining terms precisely helps brings about clarity; otherwise it's easy to get lost since a term may imply so-and-so to one person while it implies such-and-such to another.

Thoughts

For the purposes of this book a thought is defined as an idea, composed of language, which deals with anything outside the immediate present. Although not always obvious, thought requires language. The purpose of language is to transmit meaning in a symbolic and succinct manner. Like thought itself, language is always about some thing: it is not—and can not—be the thing itself. For instance, if a person sees a swastika, he might think, "Nazi symbol." Another person might think, "Ancient Indian symbol." Yet another might think, "Strange cross." Of course, it is none of these; it is simply a swastika. In fact, it is not even that (for "swastika" is another word). In actuality, it is simply what it is. The words, meanings or thoughts about it are another matter altogether.

Each thought involves summoning or creating a convenient translation of the object of its attention. After a while, though, it's easy to mistake the translation for the original object itself. This is the power of association, and is one of the traits that makes thought so compelling.

(There is a type of cognition which entails summoning or creating mental images—representational thinking—but these are also subtly imbued with word-meaning. In deep concentration, sometimes the word-meaning is overcome and then thought is transcended.)

The mind manufactures thoughts continuously; more than the average person is aware. Most people aren't conscious of the extent to which their minds produce an ongoing stream of thought: daydreams, memories, plans, hopes, concerns, monologues and dialogues, beliefs, and more. This stream is so constant there seems to be little point in paying much attention to it; we take it for granted and it's become largely inconspicuous. If you ask someone, "What are you thinking?" they may honestly respond, "Nothing." But this answer likely stems from low self-awareness on their part. Most of us are "asleep at the wheel" when it comes to being aware of our thought processes; for instance, even when paying attention to our thinking, we are mainly aware of the main thoughts and not the background component thoughts that lead to them—we see the cake but don't know the ingredients. We also tend to not notice that our thoughts never pertain to our present moment.

This may sound peculiar to some readers, and they might say, "But I can think about the present. I can think about what is happening here and now." It may appear that way, but in truth it's impossible. There is certainly cognition in the here and now. There are perception, awareness, and experience; but these aren't thought. Although it's been equated with intelligence and even with our very being ("I think, therefore I am"), thinking is only one expression of consciousness. A thought is made up of language (an artificial and acquired trait), and the mind thus has to reach into its memory banks to produce it; this takes time. But there is no time to think in the now. While thought occurs *in* the present, it can't really be *about* the present because by the time you produce a thought about the present, that present has quickly become the past.

Thoughts, Feelings, and Behaviors

The same goes for the here; there is no space to think about.

Living your life isn't the same as thinking about living your life. Let's suppose you're having a wonderful time with your friends; all the while you are perceiving and experiencing this series of life moments and the sensations and feelings that go with it. But the moment you say to yourself, "Ah, what a great time I'm having," that's a thought. Although it happens very rapidly, you have to mentally remove yourself from a situation to think about it. Thinking sets up a sort of filter between you and reality.

You can buy a Ferrari or you can think about buying a Ferrari. You can date a beautiful woman or you can think about dating a beautiful woman. You can love and respect yourself or you can think about loving and respecting yourself.

Ultimately, there is a theoretical quality to thought, as opposed to the truthful quality most people suppose it has. Many of us are very fond of our thoughts. We tend to assume that just because we think something, it must be true or valid somehow. If you think, "A gigantic live blue bunny rabbit is about to fly through my front door," and picture it in your mind, that hardly means it's going to happen. While it may be argued this is a fantastic thought, the example nevertheless shows how thinking isn't tantamount to reality. And yet when many people think to themselves, "I'm a loser," they believe it is necessarily so.

Because a thought can never *be* those things which it concerns itself with, it has no realistic status of its own, aside from really being a thought. That is, a thought is only real as a symbol. If I write the word "cat" on a slip of paper, this is not the same as a cat. And if I burn that slip of paper, I'm not burning a cat. But nevertheless the word "cat" is real as a symbol; it's really a word even if it's not really a cat.

Thoughts also play a subtle physical role as neurological energies that symbolize or translate the phenomena which they are attending to, but it's helpful to always distinguish between thoughts and their subject or object. Between mentality and reality.

Feelings

When we look into the second of the three psychological components—feelings—we note a fundamental difference. Thoughts work with the brain; they are intellectual and relatively abstract. But feelings (synonymous with emotions) are the *body's* response to thoughts.

Emotions are often confused with thoughts and so may seem less bodily than they are. Yet in English the word "feeling" is used both for strictly physical feelings (heat, stiffness, aches, comfort) *and* emotional feelings (love, anger, joy, fear). Emotional feelings are more subtle than purely physical ones (which everyone realizes are in the body) and, as an explicit and often very rapid response to thoughts, their frequent confusion with thoughts is understandable.

The fact that emotions are experienced throughout the body makes them more vivid and challenging than thoughts. There's nothing theoretical about an emotion, nor is it an intellectual exercise. It is felt *because* it's pulsing with unpredictable life energy: our body is telling us what it makes of our thoughts.

It's easy for a woman to think, "I'm not afraid of speaking in public. I have a good command of language and I know my topic. Besides, the audience is just a bunch of individuals, and if I'm not scared to talk to each one alone, why should I be scared to speak to all of them together?" But when the moment comes to step out in front of the audience, she may be overcome with panic. Why? She has likely had many negative thoughts about public speaking that outweigh these few positive ones she came up with, and her emotions have been cumulatively affected.

Thoughts create the context or frame for feelings to respond to. This isn't always apparent. If someone stubs their toe into a table and, in pain, feels frustrated and angry, it might seem like the frustration and anger are in response to the physical pain caused by the accident. But this isn't the case. The emotions are in response to the *meaning* of the event; and meaning is a thought trait. For example, if a masochist stubs his toe, the pain might be welcome; hence, no frustration and anger but pleasure instead.

There's no particular correlation between events and feelings, but between the meanings of events and feelings. A man comes home one day and finds his wife in bed with his best friend. The "normal" response is to be overcome with feelings of anger, hate, jealousy, sadness, and so on, maybe even resulting in homicide or suicide. But what if the man in question has a swinger's sensibility, with values more libertine than those of normal society? He might chuckle at the scene. Aroused, he might then ask to join in. Or he may sincerely request they give him a video of their lovemaking. Different meaning, different feelings.

Like thoughts, many feelings are semi-conscious; it's as though they're hiding, laying in wait, ready to spring forth when some cue—personal or environmental—triggers them.

Behaviors

While feelings are in the body, behaviors are done *with* the body. Synonymous with actions, they are the body's visible response to thoughts and feelings.

Everything that can be done with the body is a behavior: walking on the beach, eating an orange, sleeping on a futon, listening to the radio, smelling fresh-baked bread, and watching a sunrise are some examples.

Some people may object, "Sleeping isn't a behavior. He's just laying there unconscious. He's not *doing* anything!" It may not be the most externally active behavior, but it is nevertheless an act. To sleep is to do something. And though it may appear non-active, it requires the coordination and cooperation of the mind, emotions, and body. Just ask anyone with insomnia.

Because behaviors are so overtly physical (since they require the body's participation), they are in a sense an even greater challenge than feelings. Even more than feelings, behaviors are utterly grounded in "real life." If I *feel* anxious training for a sky-diving jump, how much harder will it be to actually *do* the jump itself?

Although the physicality of behaviors makes them challenging, it also endows them with a tangibility and sense of accomplishment that is very therapeutic. It's often less daunting (and more rewarding) to do things than to think about doing them or bother with our feelings about them. Instead of spending all month nervous and frightened about my visit to the dentist, isn't it more useful to go to my appointment and get it done? Instead of being a recluse for fear of rejection, isn't it healthier to go out and associate with others to share their company?

Yes, these options are more simple and sound. But thought often interferes and complicates things unnecessarily. Since feelings and behaviors answer to the meanings created by thought, they get distressed to the extent that thoughts are faulty: if our thinking is neurotic or unrealistic, then our emotions and behaviors just go along for the ride. So the value of mind managing's key feature—learning to understand thought and set it in its proper place—becomes more apparent.

Chapter 3
The Personality

In the previous chapter, we examined the role of thoughts, feelings, and behaviors. We indicated how these three factors are significant in the daily lives of all people, and how each person is aware of them—to one degree or another—from experience and observation. We also indicated how the only one of the three that is rational (thought) is itself limited in its ability to interpret reality; that, in fact, all it can do is create a symbolic translation of reality which is convenient and useful. (As an aside, thought, being by nature a tool, is not really intelligent or conscious per se, but is guided by the intelligence in the will. Similarly, we don't say that a brush painted a picture, but that an artist painted it—with the use of a brush.)

Every human life consists of a long stream of

relatively interconnected thoughts, feelings, and behaviors. This particular history of psychological traits forms our character or biography. The part we play in the life drama. What I am describing here is not really synonymous with our Self, in the sense of an individual in his or her entirety, but with our personality*. From the Greek *persona,* meaning "mask." This root implies that the word "person" refers to a covering, a role we inhabit.

We all put this persona on every morning.

The personality acts as the outer layer of the Self. This layer is where culture generally teaches us to place our attention and values, and with good reason; it's the layer that directly faces the external world and mediates its concerns. We need a personality. Otherwise, what are we going to present to everyone, a blank? In fact, the main function of the personality is to help us deal with society as a coherent, tangible character. It thinks, feels, and behaves, but not just that: it thinks, feels, and behaves with a certain self-defining consistency. It has a name (usually first listed on our birth certificate), a physical body, a life story, a style, and a series of traits; many

---

*The Self—with a capital "s"—may be defined as the whole human being, including the personal (ego) and universal (will) selves.

memories, plans, opinions and beliefs; habits and preferences; aptitudes and skills; and is friends with other personalities. It's the me character I know and play and who stars in *The Me Show,* produced, written, and directed by me with help from friends, family, society, and nature.

Though it's the outermost aspect of our Self, the personality is under the impression that it alone is the whole Self. It's that part of us which has forgotten our other parts and doesn't know it has forgotten them. In a sense, it has been tricked. And because it meets society's needs, we are—from earliest childhood—reinforced on an almost constant basis to identify with it. It absorbs our sense of self. This identification becomes so entrenched, it can then feel very uncomfortable to detach from it.

We each love our personality. Even when we hate it, we love it. Or maybe we don't love it; maybe we just need it and so cling to it. Or maybe we only think we need it: because we think it's the whole us.

This over-identification is the main dilemma posed by the personality. It's as though all the Self's eggs have been placed in the personality's little basket and the Self is now very worried about that basket. This stance produces a sense of vulnerability. Being entranced by outer concerns (by how well it and its body go through the external world), the personality depends on them for security and its sense of worth. Everything is generally fine as long as nothing potentially hurtful happens; but the moment an event occurs that our personality deems hurtful (by giving it a negative or threatening meaning), it begins to judge and resist the event. And the disharmony starts.

Life can be, and often is, cruel to the personality. Whenever you see someone in sorrow or distress, that's their personality. For instance, if a man comes home and finds that his house has been vandalized and looted, his personality may suffer pangs of rage, depression, denial, and disgust. But if he were to adopt the viewpoint of his will (or of his Self), his perspective would be less narrow and he'd be less dependent on the desirability or undesirability of the situation before him. He may then not even be phased; he may even be mildly amused. And not from any attempt to deny his misfortune, but from a greater understanding that takes more factors into account and clearly perceives the larger picture. (As opposed to just imagining idealistic or wishful thoughts.)

But the personality—a more limited and narrow-minded thing—typically feels threatened and hurt over such an unfortunate situation. It has so little knowledge of the real meanings and lessons in difficult life events, that it resists them and causes itself much strife and pain. Pain which may never be fully overcome or healed (while viewed from the ego's perspective).

Even once an event is over, the personality keeps thinking about it. Judging it. Cursing it. Regretting it. Fearing it. Even if I am now completely safe and secure, my mind will likely continue pondering it, disappointed in its occurrence, nervous about its recurrence. The event is finished. I have survived it. I could be thinking about 1,001 other things, many of which in all likelihood are more entertaining and relevant. So why the conflict? Why do I upset myself like this? One part of my mind creates a problem and the other part frets about the problem that the first part created. It's a mental civil war.

How did this irrational obsession over hurtful events start? One thing psychologists have confirmed is that when you reject or avoid something that is disagreeable but natural or necessary, it tends to become more imposing.

The Role of Emotional Pain and Pleasure

Because of its limited cognitive scope, the personality gambles all its security on the status of its identity as judged by itself; and to bolster this status, it *resists emotional hurt* and *invites emotional pleasure*. These two strategies sound reasonable, at least on the surface (domain of the personality). But analyzed more closely, they are seen to be mental habits developed by people over the centuries but derived from a natural-selection principle common in the animal kingdom.

The avoidance of bodily pain's causes and the pursuit of bodily pleasure have a biological survival basis: these behaviors are fundamentally self-protective and tend to increase one's safety, and by extension that of one's species, since they attempt to maintain the integrity and well-being of the body. But it appears that, at some point in history, people began adapting this survival mechanism that was intended for the body and transferring it onto their psychological lives.

Emotional pain and pleasure, which are constructed more or less arbitrarily by the mind through its meaning-making, thus became increasingly dominant concerns. The thrust of the original instinct for the *body's* protection was, "Be afraid to have a tiger's jaws around your neck, but desire to eat well and have sex." What the mind gradually made of this for the *personality's* survival was, "Be afraid of fearful or hurt feelings and distract yourself from them whenever possible, including by overindulging your appetites."

The biological instinct was likely applied to the emotional sphere because it must have seemed then (as it often does even today) a practical and attractive way to manage fear and distress. But aversion to psychological pain, and fixation on psychological pleasure, don't help the personality survive so as much as limit it. By declining to feel genuine emotional pain, people become less apt to feel genuine emotional pleasure. The ability to feel both is one and the same. Distancing themselves from their emotional pain, it seems increasingly foreboding; they grow more afraid of it and so turn more desperately to heightened pleasure for solace, which helps rob it of its spontaneity and joy. It's a lose-lose proposition. On the other hand, when they allow themselves to feel their own hurt or fear, even cherishing it as a life sensation, their ability to feel good increases in response. Emotional range and strength grow.

This is not to say we should seek out pain and shun pleasure. But when an occasion occurs in which *either* emotional pain *or* pleasure is a natural response, then the feeling should be honored and experienced fully. Disharmony comes from not being open to both.

Incidentally, this is similar to the fear of life and death. If you are very afraid to die, you are also afraid to live your life for fear that something may kill you.

To not deal with a hurt feeling, the mind typically engages in numerous convolutions and contortions. Justifications are created, and beliefs developed, to deny or minimize a hurt whose true significance must now be ignored. It takes a lot of energy to maintain this strategy, which can last for years if the hurt has a meaning that threatens the personality. Unfortunately, the personality's mania toward "survival" for its own sake makes it keep the pain covered, discouraging healing.

The next chapter discusses methods used by the personality to maintain this imbalanced way of operating.

Chapter 4
Choice of Mind

It's often been said that the mind can be your best friend or worst enemy. This is true enough, and which one it will be depends on what kind of relationship you're developing with it. While the mind is meant to be ably managed by its owner, this is usually the result of persistently practicing positive psychological habits while relinquishing negative ones, like so shaping and training the mind. (I'm referring here to the conscious—sensing and thinking—mind. The superconscious mind, or will, can't be managed because it's much vaster than the ego. But the personality can be receptive and willing to understand the superconscious.)

I think that the conscious mind is a lot like a horse. When untamed, a horse is wild and unruly; if you try to get on, it throws you off violently. It won't let you near it and it certainly won't work for you. However, once tamed, the horse lets you on and takes you where you want. It works with you in a spirit of mutual benefit.

Many people have little or no control over what they think, feel, or do. Their minds do the driving and they just go along for the ride, unable or unwilling to steer their own course. They probably don't know they can be in better control. For here culture has let them down: they haven't been taught that they are greater than their minds; that they are rightfully the boss.

To be at the mercy of your mind is as desirable as being at the mercy of, say, your hands. Like the mind, hands are a useful part of you. You respect your hands, take care of them, and use them every day. But they are there to do what you want. Can you imagine how troublesome it would be if you had little or no control over them? What if your hands suddenly decided to slap you in the face? Or strangle you? Or give your neighbor the finger? If your hands were beyond your power to control, each day would be an anxiety-provoking odyssey. You'd have to constantly be on guard, lest your hands decided to do something unpredictable and wrong.

Without doubt, the conscious mind is a very important part of you, but a part can never be greater than the whole to which it belongs. Hands are also wonderful, but can anyone honestly say their hands are greater than them and should be in charge?

The Two Aspects

Broadly speaking, there are two aspects to the conscious mind; the healthy one is called the *active* aspect, the unhealthy one is known as the *passive-reactive* aspect. Every person has both, and the differences between people's degrees of mental health arise from the extent to which one or the other aspect is emphasized by them. Most people blend them more or less equally, resulting in what is called "normality," meaning the average person who usually functions at what society deems an acceptable level. He or she could be doing much better but could also be a lot worse off. This person hasn't achieved full potential but yet resists utter dysfunctionality.

At some point, you may have observed that when it comes to psychological well-being some people are exceptionally healthy and positive, others profoundly unhealthy and negative, and perhaps the majority fall somewhere in the middle. But have you ever asked yourself why this is? Factors such as genetics, organicity, socio-economic status, race, geographic location, culture, family upbringing, traumatic experience, medical health—none of these is definitive in determining a person's mental life stance because for each case of a person succumbing to one or more of these factors, there is an example of someone who ably managed and overcame the difficulty. Even more, there are people who have no problematic factors in their lives and are very negative, while others have numerous problems and are very positive.

The true variable, then, can't be found in the problems themselves but in the psychological responses to them.

Because the two aspects exist in all people, they are completely normal in and of themselves. In one way or another, everyone experiences them all the time; we each have our light and dark sides, our highs and lows. But just because something is normal or natural doesn't make it healthy. Normal simply means "of the norm" or "common." So, presuming that the goal is to be psychologically healthy (and not just normal), we need to learn how to stimulate the active aspect and tame the passive-reactive aspect.

We can't rid ourselves of the passive-reactive aspect, any more than the planet can rid itself of thunder and lightning. Nor is it necessary to do so. Because it's only unhealthy to the extent that it controls us, it's enough to learn how to manage it. Probably the most effective way of doing this is to make progress in working the active aspect.

The active aspect is that side of your mind or personality which is assertive, intelligent, and energetic. You feature it when you're confident and content with who you are, express yourself directly and to the point, come up with solutions, act courageously, and analyze things rationally. The active aspect is knowing, logical, and clear-minded. It has intuition and insight, and is motivated to do what is fitting and what the demands of a given situation indicate. Strong and spontaneous, it has no particular need to attract attention or create drama.

You could be a violent, paranoid drug addict who spends most of his days thieving and his nights laying in an alley shooting dope. You still have the active aspect of your mind; but, not being used by you, it lies latent.

The passive-reactive aspect is that side of your mind or personality which is weak, stupid, and continuously hurt. You feature it when you're hating, fearing, or doubting yourself and/or others, and when you're hanging on to pain by refusing to face it. The passive-reactive aspect is highly emotional, focusing especially on anger, guilt, and self-pity. It perceives very primitively and superficially, often drawing unwarranted conclusions from the sparsest and most misleading cues. It's motivated to do whatever maintains its own status quo, regardless of whether it is right or wrong, wise or idiotic. Impulsive and insecure, it has a marked need to attract attention (usually of the negative type) and create drama.

If you're a productive, creative and energetic person who is a leader and role model in the community, of service to others, you still have the passive-reactive aspect; but, not being highlighted by you, it's inert.

Someone who mostly uses their active aspect is typically mature, stable and lucid, and projects genuine self-regard and assertiveness; one who mostly uses their passive-reactive aspect is usually immature, unstable and either neurotic or psychotic. When people use expressions like "He's out of his mind" or "She's lost her mind," they are in effect saying that person has abandoned his or her active aspect of mind.

The aspect is called "active," as opposed to "passive," because it has energy and initiative. It's a center of influence, personal power, and independence. Alert and curious, it is characterized by an unpretentious—even noble—attitude, and is firmly anchored in the present.

It's called "active," as opposed to "reactive," because it's aware and secure during challenging situations, maintaining presence of mind instead of losing emotional control as happens in reactivity. Not letting others provoke its response, it selects and enacts the response it finds most appropriate at that time.

On the other hand, the passive-reactive aspect also has a lot of power—the power to weaken—which we tend to give it when we don't know any better. We then feel maladjusted or ill at ease with life and ourselves. This aspect is quite formidable since it takes much negative energy to hold down a human being.

In movies or cartoons, we often see a character who is trying to decide what to do, and a little devil guy appears over one shoulder and tempts him to do something very wrong but which nevertheless would be immediately gratifying. A little angel guy then appears over the other shoulder to balance him out, appealing to his reason and showing him the broader picture beyond just the short-term consequences. This type of scene symbolizes the choice each of us often faces: do I take a step in the direction of health or disease?

People have often made this choice into a moral issue; but morality, which judges actions (and their actors) to be good or bad, isn't the main interest here. That's more the province of the preacher and priest. We are instead concerned whether something is healthy or unhealthy to oneself and others. If healthy, we cultivate it; if unhealthy, we don't. But by working the active aspect, we don't ignore or suppress the passive-reactive; rather, we reinforce the clarity and strength that help us understand it and put it in its rightful place.

When we realize we can empower either the active or passive-reactive aspect by how we use our minds, we begin to understand how much *responsibility* we have over our lives. Am I suggesting that having responsibility for our lives, including our problems, means we're at fault somehow? No, it's not a question of fault. People aren't necessarily responsible for what happens to them, but they are responsible for how they manage themselves and their responses, which is within their ability to choose. Responsibility means power. If you say you aren't responsible for your life, you're saying you have no power over your life.

Frequently using the active aspect earns us our connectedness, and sense of potential. Gradually, it becomes easier to face the passive-reactive aspect's issues and strategies: we comfortably acknowledge them because they don't seem as impressive as before. We see better how our psychological problems were developed and maintained by passive-reactivity—our guilt, anger, hate, self-pity, fear and sadness being states to keep our ego dominant and thus designed to not be satisfactorily resolved on their own.

As long as we played the game at that (passive-reactive) level, we couldn't really resolve our problems. It was only when we played our own game, from our own level, that we got the right perspective and could play to win.

If someone was drowning in quicksand and you wanted to save them, would you prefer to do it from within the quicksand or from a secure position on solid ground?

Chapter 5
Knowing the Obstacles

Even as you develop, the passive-reactive aspect still presents difficulties and challenges along the way. In a sense, it's testing you to make sure your progress is "for real." It helps to be fully cognizant of this tendency; the better you recognize it, the more ably you can manage it. Recognizing obstacles while they're at work is a sign of progress since otherwise they can operate freely and without interference.

This chapter introduces the main passive-reactive obstacles, which in turn will be explored more fully in Chapters 6, 7, and 8.

Two Types of Problems

In the first place, when talking about mental health,

we need to distinguish between the two kinds of problems that life offers: *psychological* and *realistic*. Psychological problems are those created by the mind, while realistic problems are those presented by external circumstances. The distinction is important because many people are under the impression that "having problems" is a sign of mental illness or that something is wrong with them.

In this book, we are mostly concerned with identifying, managing, and resolving psychological problems. We aren't as interested in realistic problems because this type of problem has nothing to do with our mental health status. A person can be absolutely healthy in the mental or emotional sense—a model of stability, insight, and contentment—and still have problems at any moment in life. He or she could go bankrupt, be evicted, become ill, lose a loved one, be punched in the face, or get into an accident. These are simply life occurrences and they may happen to anyone. They are not necessarily a result of poor psychological functioning, and in fact often have nothing to do with it. For these reasons, we are mainly addressing those problems our minds make; by learning enough about them, we can handle them better and even prevent them.

But when realistic problems happen, it's important to try our best to analyze them and, if possible, solve them; if this isn't possible, we can learn to accept them.

Often, that proves just as satisfying. If you accept a problem, and can now live with it harmoniously, just exactly how much of a problem is it?

There is nothing wrong with having realistic problems. It's not a sign of mental dysfunction. In fact, a problem is a solution in disguise. When we find the solution, the problematic aspect is over: we say that the problem is *solved*. It functions as an opportunity to increase our understanding. Psychological problems are also solutions in disguise. The difference is simply that they arise from our own minds, and not from outer circumstances.

Let's look more closely at the difference between psychological and realistic problems.

Suppose a man is invited to a party. He knows and likes the people throwing the party, as well as the invited guests, and so agrees to attend. But then he hears that the host has a Yorkshire terrier puppy. Having a phobia of dogs, regardless of size or breed, he becomes nervous and phones back the host with an excuse, explaining that he can't go.

Psychological or realistic problem? The answer, of course, is "psychological" because the man's problem is caused by his thoughts and feelings about dogs. The dog here in question poses no *realistic* danger to him and so can not be the problem.

Another example. Suppose a man travels to the

Grand Canyon and is taking photos of the views. He approaches the ledge of a cliff to get a better look, slips, and falls over the edge. As he falls, he happens to barely hold onto the edge. He is now hanging on by his fingertips, above a 4,000-foot drop to the jagged rocks below.

Is the problem psychological or realistic? Naturally, it is realistic for the man finds himself in a dangerous, and possibly deadly, situation. It's not caused by his thoughts or feelings, nor is it a product of how he perceives the matter. The situation was occasioned by an accident, such as could happen to anyone, and now it's a matter of finding the solution. For instance, he could try to pull himself up or call out for help.

Whenever you have a problem, ask yourself, "Is this problem psychological or realistic?" This will save a lot of time and energy because identifying the type tells you whether the source of the problem is in your mind or outer circumstances. And that's a clue to where the solution lies.

Because people tend to give lots of validity to their own thoughts and feelings, it often appears to them that their psychological problems are realistic. They matter-of-factly assign a reality status to their psychological problems that simply isn't there. What they believe seems so *true,* what they want seems so *necessary,* what they fear seems so *terrible.* It may not occur to them that other people don't see it this way, and that therefore they don't have to either. They have not yet identified the difference between reality and mentality.

But that's not to say there is no relation between the two. It often happens that psychological dysfunction worsens, or even wholly creates, realistic problems. A paranoid person can induce others to really dislike him and even plot against him. Or someone's poor impulse control may cause her to act out and be arrested. Conversely, realistic dilemmas can provoke psychological problems. For instance, a man finds that his home was destroyed by a hurricane and feels increasingly depressed. This interaction between the two problem types is even more grounds for learning to distinguish between them. Otherwise, we can compound our difficulties by unwittingly making psychological problems out of realistic problems and vice-versa.

The daily news provides enough evidence of how problems can cross over and spiral out of control. A typical scenario is the disgruntled ex-employee who returns to the job site and shoots up the place before turning the gun on himself. This usually involves taking a realistic problem (being fired from work) and making a psychological problem (unmanaged anger) out of it. Why would someone create an additional problem for himself, especially if it's a hundred times worse than the original? For one thing, the passive-reactive aspect loves the drama, and, if unchecked, can cause much havoc to get it.

What it comes down to is that a psychological problem is not a true problem. Or, to be more precise, it's as true as the thoughts which make it. A psychological problem *is* the thoughts which make it.

Once we understand this, we realize that our minds shouldn't be making meaning out of things without our consent. But to reach this state of mind managing, we first need to study how our mind operates. We especially need to be on the lookout for the passive-reactive aspect and its ways; the more aware we are, the less power it has over us since it can't sneak up on us so easily. We need to be vigilant like a sentry. If the guard on duty is alert, the enemy can't easily sneak into the compound; but if he's distracted or asleep, the enemy can come in unopposed and cause all kinds of difficulty.

The Passive-Reactive Obstacles

It's the passive-reactive aspect's job to sow disharmony across all three psychological manifestations—thoughts, feelings, and behaviors. It arouses problem feelings and behaviors that reinforce problem thoughts. Suppose you have a *thought*—"It's dangerous to go outside, day or night." You may then begin to *feel* nervous and frightened, and *behave* accordingly: you start staying in as much as possible, arrange to have your meals delivered, and hire an assistant to shop for you. The problem thought is now more validated than before, and more entrenched in your life.

In each manifestation, different psychological phenomena act as the obstacles to personal growth:

Manifestation	*Obstacles*
Thought	opinions, beliefs
Feeling	fear, pain, guilt
Behavior	avoidance, habit

The passive-reactive aspect is our own "worst enemy." In war, it's always advisable to know your enemy; be aware of his strengths and weaknesses, his methods and resources, his purpose. This type of assessment is productive. On the other hand, there's no point in hating your enemy because to hate something is to give it lots of time, energy and importance for little return. This inappropriately reinforces it. In addition, it's blinding to oneself. It's better to respect your opponent, even while trying your best to defeat him. In the case of the mind, this is even more necessary since hating your passive-reactive aspect means you are hating a part of yourself; also, since hate is a typical passive-reactive emotion, hating the passive-reactive aspect paradoxically results in its strengthening itself.

We can listen to our passive-reactive aspect with a neutral attitude of detached curiosity and some healthy regard. With this unbiased stance, we can more calmly recognize its influence in our daily lives, objectively see how it works, and bring it under our guidance since it will gradually seem less strange and imposing. This friendly strategy helps us develop our most natural and optimal state, in which our mind is our "best friend," and reminds us that the mind—in both its active and passive-reactive aspects—is our tool to work with.

Let's analyze more closely the mental, emotional and behavioral obstacles to personal growth.

Chapter 6
Understanding the Mental Obstacles

The mental obstacles consist of particular passive-reactive thoughts, so to understand them we first need to understand thought itself. The very nature of thought presents us with a fundamental psychological problem; namely, our tendency to be misled by the notion that our thoughts about reality are the same as reality. Analyzing thought more closely, we will see that mistaking a bunch of words or ideas for reality is like mistaking a book about Spain for Spain itself.

The Language of Thought

What's the purpose of thought? Since thought is made up of language, let's search there for the answer. Language was invented for people to communicate knowledge to one another. First came spoken language. If a woman saw a hyena approaching her mate from behind, she needed to warn him and make him see what she saw so he could protect himself. But, not being telepathic, she had to quickly transfer this knowledge to him in another way. And so spoken language developed. People began agreeing that certain sounds stood for certain things. Now, instead of grunting, which might mean any number of things, the woman could say, "Honey, hyena at six o'clock." This was much more specific and informative. Written language came later to preserve knowledge for future use.

Notice that in this explanation there's nothing about using language silently for oneself (what we today call "thinking"). Language developed because it served the necessary social function of sharing information. It was not originally designed for inner personal use, and it was no idle luxury. It was learned and utilized for communication with others. Why would one need to silently communicate words to oneself?

You already know what *you* know. Do you need to translate it into words for yourself, in your mind? Let's suppose a woman has to go shopping at the supermarket. That is all. She knows it. She can then just go shopping. But, no, most likely she'll think, "Oh-I-need-to-go-shopping-at-the-supermarket-today." Why does she have to use all those words? Or any words at all? Is she afraid she won't know what to do unless she says them to herself? Even if she isn't a mind reader, she can easily know what's on her own mind and what her needs are without having to enunciate them to herself. Thinking in words is like translating a conversation between two people who speak the same language.

Somewhere along the line, humanity cultivated this habit of using language silently for self-communication, instead of just for social interaction. This shows how the external side of life has colored the internal. And thinking became more and more established. It may originally have been an attempt at self-consolation due perhaps to boredom, loneliness, or insecurity. Note that some people talk to themselves *aloud,* which is similar to thinking except it's externalized and even less necessary.

Not Thinking

One problem with thinking is it uses lots of energy. Our minds produce thousands of thoughts daily, and studies show that for most people a large percentage of them is the same, day in and day out. It's like having TV reruns in your head. Again and again, we tell ourselves what we like or want, remind ourselves of what we fear and hate, and entertain ourselves with fantasies and memories. It would be kind of nice, except that this constant thinking is largely unproductive and ultimately tiring for mind and body. Imagine that every time you need to do something or go somewhere, you have to think about it first. Then you think about it some more while you're doing it. After, you can think about what you did. And about what you plan to do later. And so on.

Wouldn't it be easier to just do it, whatever *it* is? If you need to go to the bathroom, why think, "I need to go to the bathroom"? You can just know it ("!") and go. This is tantamount to having wordless thought: the pure idea before it gets translated into language.

Remember that language is inefficient for self-communication because that's not what it's for. It was designed to be shared with others.

So why think at all? A valid question. Undoubtedly, thought has certain applications. Aside from its value in communication, it's an effective way to organize and review the knowledge you've gained from society since most of this knowledge is in linguistic form anyway. Also, since thought doesn't deal with the present, it's helpful for remembering the past and planning for the future; this helps orient you toward society's needs and you thus feel better adjusted. In addition, thought supports the personality and gives it its structure, which is helpful for having coherent and ordered dealings with others throughout life. (As long as you have a body, you will have a personality; but that doesn't mean the personality should take over your life. Ideally, the personality is guided by your will.)

It's not that thought is a bad thing; it just needs to be put in its rightful place. It's become our foreman when it's really our toolbox.

The amount we think could be reduced to our benefit. Taking breaks from chronic thinking helps us refresh; we lose less energy than usual. If someone always left their car engine on, it would soon burn out. How important for the engine to rest. And yet we keep our minds going with thought the whole day, every day. While the body and brain get some rest through sleep, our thoughts often continue unconsciously and influence our dreams. At any rate, sleep doesn't solve the problem because it can't keep us from losing energy during the waking day.

Practicing non-thinking helps you experience life aside from thought and learn you can be independent of it. You notice the limitations of thought and take it less seriously; there is less pressure. You may still respect it as an important mental process but no longer consider its creations to definitely be synonymous with truth.

Correct Thinking

Besides non-thinking (or wordless thought), it's valuable to know how to think as ably as possible. Since thought is both inevitable and necessary, thinking correctly is a worthwhile skill. Correct thinking has nothing to do with being right; it just means thinking that is lucid, precise and rational and knows the limitations of thought itself. This last quality is vital because reason—no matter how impeccably logical and factual—can not capture an absolute truth. It's a key cognitive error of some very rational persons to mistake their ideas or thoughts for such truths.

To help you develop correct thinking, we will first review certain qualities of language and, second, identify and compare the various types of thought (and what they do) so that you may more easily distinguish between them. Let's proceed.

Recognizing that thought is made up of language, it's in your interest to be very alert to the words you engage each day. Words form your ideas as well as your understanding of *you* and your life; they shape how you perceive reality itself. The more aware you are of how this works, the better you can manage it.

For example, a man tells his physician, "Doc, I can't quit smoking." This is a common saying for smokers: their health is failing them and they know they should quit; perhaps they tried to several times but went back. And yet the saying is utterly false. First off, it contains what I call the c-word: *can't*. This word is a contraction for "can not." It means something can *not* be done; that it is impossible for this something to be done by this person, at least at this time. And yet the word *can't* is

Understanding the Mental Obstacles 49

abused all the time. It's often applied to those things that literally *can* be done. O, correct language, where are you? If a woman says, "I can't lift 800 pounds with one arm" or "I can't fly away like a bird and travel to a moon crater," she is using *can't* accurately since these things are impossible for her.

What the smoker *really* means is, "Doc, I don't want to quit smoking."

Let's consider this example of the smoker in more detail and note how words can trip us up and affect our lives.

When a smoker thinks he *can't* quit smoking, he tells himself he's incapable of doing what is necessary to quit. For whatever reason, this is his idea and he may live many disempowering years believing it. Curiously, the idea is all wrong. In the first place, there's nothing to *do* in order to quit smoking. You don't have to go anywhere or buy anything. Quitting smoking only involves *not doing* something you are used to doing. This means not doing many things—no longer spending money on cigarettes, cracking open a pack, getting a light, inhaling and exhaling smoke, asking others for a smoke, and so on. How can you not *not do* something?

In the newspaper you'll often see a headline such as "U.S. Breaks Relations with India." The U.S. (United States) is a land mass of 3,536,278 square miles with over 300 million people, while India is a land mass of

1,246,880 square miles with over 900 million people. But the headline is saying the first land mass and its people broke relations with the second land mass and all *its* people. In reality, nothing of the sort happened. What did happen was that a small group of politicians (president, vice-president, secretary of state, and so on) decided to break diplomatic relations with the political leaders in charge of the government of India; basically, it's a tiff between two groups of chief civil servants. But the headline makes it appear that the situation is much more definite and widespread—and inevitable—than it really is.

Though we understand (when we stop to consider it) that these are just expressions for the sake of convenience, they still subtly mold our attitudes and expectations. Even if we know they're not literally true, they influence our minds, often to the extent of limiting our potential or understanding in some way. They act as signals that play to our perceptions and emotions. This shouldn't really be surprising since we all know that the everyday choices we have for words, even for saying what is essentially the same thing, are fraught with consequences. A nurse saying either "I need a stool sample from you" or "I need a piece of your shit" would draw very different responses from a patient.

One example that directly affects mental health is when people say something like, "I'm depressed." My favorite response to this is, "Pleased to meet you, depressed. I'm Alex." It's not widely known but no one in the history of this planet has ever been depressed. It's simply not possible to be depressed. Or to be depression. You can, however, *feel* depressed. If someone feeling sad, hopeless, and fatigued said, "I feel depressed," she would be sticking to the facts. If that's what you feel, you may choose to say so. But feeling (or thinking) something is different from being it. Being is "what you are" and alludes to your very self. At its core, your identity has duration, a sense of longevity. On the other hand, feelings are like clouds: they come, stay awhile, and then go (especially if you let them). They are not you but something you do, and which at any time you might stop doing. How wise is it to equate these transient feeling states with your being? A person can't *be* anything other than him- or herself. To say, "I am hungry," "I am happy," "I am Italian" or "I am a Yankees fan" is to identify with a word or label. We tell ourselves we *are* that thing and equate ourselves with it. The problem? It's not true so we mislead ourselves with a false impression.

Facts and Judgments

The two basic types of thought are *facts* and *judgments*. Facts are statements that accurately describe something. Judgments are statements that describe how much or how little we *like* that something. Facts, being objective, are neutral; judgments, being subjective, are biased.

Suppose a group of friends goes to a movie. Afterward, one says, *"Star Wars* is a lousy movie." Another says, *"Star Wars* is a great movie." A third says, *"Star Wars* is a movie." Which of these statements are fact and which are judgment? The first one is a negative judgment (the movie isn't liked), the second a positive judgment (the movie is liked), the third a fact (the movie's existence is acknowledged).

Judgments establish the conditions for discord; whether positive or negative, a judgment is bound to clash with its opposite. The two friends could argue for days as to the merits or faults of the movie, perhaps not grasping that, when it comes to judgments, *no one is ultimately right;* or, conversely, that everyone is right but only for him- or herself (and those who agree).

Simply put, judgments aren't factual. But note that the friends stated their judgments as though they were facts; they said the movie *is* lousy or great. The verb *to be,* in all its forms (is, was, are, am), has considerable authority since it's designed to report facts (things that *are)*. It's misleading when used to express judgments. At such times it's more fitting to add a judgmental form, for example, "I think *Star Wars* is a lousy movie" or "In my opinion, *Star Wars* is a great movie."

The third statement is a fact; it only indicates that

Star Wars is a movie. *Star Wars* meets enough criteria for what is defined as a movie: it was photographed with motion picture film, has a script, features a cast of actors, is projected onto a screen, and so on. When it comes to facts, *everyone who states them is right*. There's no such thing as a positive or negative fact—if you like or don't like a fact, that's a judgment. There is also no room for reasonable argument. It does no good to say, "*Star Wars* is a basket of vegetables." Likewise, it's futile to add a judgmental form and say, "In my opinion, *Star Wars* is a movie."

Consistently engaging in factual thought is a valid way to let go of, and prevent, psychological problems because facts streamline thought to its necessary essentials; while judgments often set up conflict and provoke overthinking. The discipline of "sticking to the facts" is a core cognitive skill.

Needless to say, the active aspect works with facts while the passive-reactive deals in judgments.

While there's only one type of fact, there are two types of judgment: *opinions* and *beliefs*. (These constitute the two key passive-reactive obstacles in thinking.) Opinions are judgments of something evident and perceivable by the five senses, while beliefs are judgments of something not in evidence—either intangible or physically absent. In the above example of the moviegoers, the judgments were opinions; they saw the movie and so could form opinions about it. Beliefs are more a matter of faith or speculation: they are like opinions, except formed without direct perception of the phenomenon in question. If someone asks you whether you think John F. Kennedy's assassination was the result of a conspiracy, your response would be a belief: for example, "Yes, I think it was a conspiracy" or "No, I don't think it was." No matter how firmly you believe it, or how right you think you are, it's a belief. Unless you were directly involved in his assassination, you don't know the facts of the matter.

When you *believe* in something, it shows you don't know it. If your name is Keith and someone asks you "Is your name Keith?" you wouldn't say "I believe so." You'd say "Yes" because you *know* your name. But how do you know? It's on your birth certificate. Your mother named you that. It's what your friends call you. You sign your name that way. It's on your license. As a fact, it's evident.

There's nothing particularly wrong with beliefs and opinions so long as we don't mistake them for factual knowledge. Unfortunately, the difference between them isn't always recognized.

Many world problems are due to this confusion between what is fact and what is judgment. Most wars—certainly all religious wars—owe their existence to it. People get emotionally invested in their ideas and so consider their mere judgments to have the weight of fact. The two types of thought have been so thoroughly blended that the error usually isn't even suspected; or else it's exploited.

When a person considers their own judgments factual, they're more likely to feel threatened when someone else expresses differing judgments; they might assume their "facts" (their understanding of reality itself) are in danger and turn defensive and aggressive, even hateful. If they realized only their judgments were being countered, they would probably feel more secure.

Stating facts as facts and judgments as judgments helps clarify things. Consider the different reactions you can elicit by telling someone, "Your god is not the true God" *(judgment stated as fact)* versus "I don't agree your god is the true God" *(judgment stated as judgment)*. The same goes for thoughts about ourselves: "I am an idiot" *(judgment stated as fact)* versus "I don't understand" *(fact stated as fact)*. Though sticking to the facts as much as possible leads to the clearest thought, it's alright to express judgments as long as you *know* they're judgments and express them accordingly.

A philosopher could argue that ultimately it isn't factual to say a hamburger is a hamburger, that a hamburger is really just a series of atomic energy charges which forms the appearance of a hamburger to our senses. While this is scientifically accurate, for everyday practical purposes (at the level of our conscious mind) we can factually say it's a hamburger. Even though it's not an absolute truth (anything stated in language can at most be only relatively true), it is sufficiently true and thus proves convenient. We are discussing things that are true only within the realm of our thought.

Similarly, mentality—the version of reality our mind gives us—is an illusion; it isn't true because it's constructed by our sensing and thinking. But just because something isn't true doesn't make it unreal. An illusion may not be true but it is real as an illusion. It really *is* an illusion. The characters and events in *The Wizard of Oz* aren't true but, within the context of the fictional story, they really happen. If they didn't, there would be no story.

So while our subjectivity (mentality) isn't the same as objectivity (reality), it has its own properties which are beneficial for us to know. Ultimately, the words we use have effects and we can use them wisely. To the extent that we think at all, let's practice discrimination and precision in the thoughts we make.

Chapter 7
Understanding the Emotional Obstacles

In some ways, feelings might be the greatest challenge on our journey of self-development. Not being rational, they seem less predictable and safe, and are often experienced as an intensely personal commotion of inner energy. Thoughts, in comparison, seem more comprehensible; by nature they have meaning. If they perturb us, we can make a little story out of them to console ourselves or put some "spin" on them with a convenient interpretation. Thoughts are remote enough that we can deny or distort them through rationalization and other defense mechanisms.

We can also try this strategy to make our feelings more pleasant, but it only delays our confronting them; it doesn't transform them or make them go away. With feelings, there's no acquittal or pardon; at most, there is a reprieve. The problem is you can't think your feelings away without causing emotional, and even physical, blockage; having a strong bodily presence, their energy is best discharged by consciously feeling it.

When people deny their emotions or are cut off from their feelings, they usually assume those feelings have disappeared somehow. That they've gone away. But where could they have gone to? Chicago? Paris? All those people have done is drive their feelings deeper into their unconscious and into their muscles and organs.

Each natural phenomenon tends to have a purpose to fulfill, and feelings are no different. Their function—their natural mission—is to be felt. The word "feelings" says it all. If it was otherwise, they might have been called "ignorings" or "suppressings."

Feelings are more primal and universal than thoughts. Animals and human infants don't think (not having acquired language) but they definitely feel. Their feelings go along with their perceptions and instincts as a sort of living commentary. If they separate from their herd or family, they may feel lonely and vulnerable; if their body hasn't had water, they may feel thirsty and anxious; if a predator or adversary approaches, they may feel afraid; if they eat a good meal, they may feel pleased and satisfied. The feelings prompt them to act in ways that help ensure their well-being and survival. A gazelle's running away from a leopard and a baby crying out for food or attention are examples. Feelings thus serve a natural function of promoting life through self-communication that leads to appropriate action.

(It may be argued that animals and human infants have language since they communicate. However, this isn't language in the developed human sense of syntax and vocabulary, but a more basic symbolic communication stimulated by instinct rather than thought.)

So if feelings are such a necessary life phenomenon, how could they ever be an obstacle? The answer is that they aren't; rather, the obstacle is in *not* feeling your emotions. "Dancing around" them prevents their resolution—it creates a gap in the flow of self-communication. Not permitted to fulfill their role, the frustrated feelings linger, getting caught up in the personality and body. Life goes on but the dissatisfied feelings remain, waiting to be felt and released from their imprisonment in your mindbody. Meanwhile, like anything else, they need to survive and so feed off your energy. Someone with a few unresolved feelings can still have plenty of vitality; but the more feelings get trapped and accumulate, the lower the vitality. Someone carrying dozens or hundreds of unfelt feelings will have less positive energy available and be left quite taxed. This blocking up of one's energy can ultimately affect a range of health areas, including concentration, self-esteem, posture, or immune strength.

The gist of feeling emotions fully is often

misunderstood at first. People sometimes object, thinking it means they'll lose to the dreaded feeling ("So if I feel scared, I'll be a coward and feel scared all the time?"). Or else they may interpret it as license to act out ("I feel angry and want to punch someone. That's okay for me to do, right?").

No and no. These overboard responses come from the passive-reactive aspect, which dramatizes problem feelings to prevent their healing and complicate any viable solutions. Anything for you not to get in touch with your emotions. For example, when people act out violently it's because they have *not* fully felt their anger. Many find this surprising. Surely, they think, a violent person must be very in touch with his anger. But—all appearances to the contrary—this is not so. It's precisely because he hasn't fully felt and resolved his anger that it controls him and moves him to commit dangerous acts. The anger is unresolved to the extent of emotionally frustrating or torturing him to desperation. So desperate that he seeks relief in some radical gesture.

But these radical gestures tend to cause more problems than they solve. In any case, unless the gesture is accompanied by feeling the problem emotion fully, any relief gained will be temporary. In itself, the radical gesture is unnecessary; more to the point, it's usually an obstacle. But such is the power of feelings that sometimes people would rather go to great extremes—even die or kill—than feel them fully. (Consider this: whenever someone commits suicide, it means they'd rather die than feel their feelings.)

Radical gestures of violence may attempt to contact and express anger, but this can be better accomplished by going into your bedroom and writing out your angry feelings and then placing the paper on a plate and burning it. This is as symbolic as a radical gesture but more effective: your anger is let out, yet nothing valuable breaks and no one gets hurt. No complications to distract you from healing.

One popular means of perpetuating troubled feelings is by identifying with them. In this case, the passive-reactive aspect uses them to mold the personality into a specially defined character: rebel, victim, tough guy, eccentric, etc. There is now a personal stake in the feelings, and pleasure is derived from them: the comfort and security of having a role to play, despite (or because of) all the difficulties they create. So it's consciously or unconsciously decided to not confront and resolve them. For if they get resolved, who would I be then? How would I spend my time? Who would I blame?

Feeling your feelings fully doesn't mean they will defeat you or run your life. On the contrary: you are taking the initiative and exercising your right to feel them. Embrace them with an attitude of respect—toward them and yourself. As you feel them to completion, you own them and take away their oppressive power, in effect neutralizing the negative energy that convinced you they were so unapproachable and scary.

This self-aware feeling shouldn't be confused with emotional drama or sentimentality. Not all feeling is created equal. Active feeling heals because there's a learning experience and it leads to progress, while passive-reactive feeling only amounts to theatre, pretending to feel but never really accessing and expressing the source of the problem.

It's a relief when you allow the release of your emotions, giving them the opportunity to fulfill their purpose and say, "Mission accomplished." It's only your mind, with its collection of arbitrary thoughts and ideas, usually learned from society, that can interfere.

The Emotional Obstacles to Your Progress

If you decide to progress psychologically, you will sooner or later need to contend with the massive amount of misinformation in your mind. Most of your thoughts really originate from society: parents, friends, neighbors, school, news media, culture, and so on. Your understanding of reality is a socially-derived phenomenon. We are all taught from a very young age what to think and feel; this may be necessary from the viewpoint of practical socialization but has little to do with real psychological health. It would be better if we were taught *how* to think and feel.

A big part of personal development (what Carl Jung called *individuation*) consists of systematically analyzing what you "know" and determining its validity for yourself. Really questioning and testing it. What usually happens is that you proceed to *unlearn* a great many of the "truths" you spent a whole lifetime learning. Some you happen to agree with and keep; others don't fit the new developing "you" and you throw them away. You start realizing that many opinionated people in your life didn't know what they were talking about. That, though in retrospect they could barely manage their own lives, they were very generous with their judgments, which were often stated in the manner of God-given facts.

When working through emotional obstacles, it helps to know that much of our own resistance and hesitation originally comes from society. It's learned. Society provides all kinds of myths, rules and cues telling us what is, or is not, okay to feel. The passive-reactive aspect then eagerly latches on to them, seizing any opportunity to validate information that can interfere with inner harmony—in this way, it has cultivated emotional obstacles designed to maintain the suppression of our feeling energy. The core emotional obstacle is *fear,* which in turn gives rise to the next two major ones, *pain* and *guilt.*

Emotional obstacles are feeling states most of us

don't like and prefer to avoid. They are the villains of the feeling world. Because they're held in such contempt and are so desperately avoided, we can right away surmise that, being feelings, they should be felt respectfully whenever the opportunity arises and that any attempt to belittle or repress them must be the work of the passive-reactive aspect. As "villains," they've been banished; now we can extend them an invitation.

Fear

Let's begin by looking at fear. Just as with problems, there are the two types of fear: *realistic* and *psychological*. Realistic fear is designed to help you avoid threats and danger: if you're afraid of situations or things that could harm you, you're more likely to avoid them and so increase your odds of surviving. That is straightforward enough. From the evolutionary standpoint, realistic fear is good. It's a sign that you care enough about your safety. Psychological fear, on the other hand, is fear caused by the meanings your mind makes. It has nothing to do with life-threatening situations, for, if it did, it would be realistic fear. Take the most common fear in the United States: fear of public speaking. The worst that could happen to a frightened speaker is that he or she would perform horribly and be laughed off the stage and left feeling greatly humiliated. But so what? That wouldn't kill them or threaten their safety in any way. Unpleasant the experience may be, but they would survive it. And all this is the *worst* that could happen.

There are many psychological fears: fear of success, failure, rejection, intimacy, being alone, open spaces, closed spaces, and on and on. You can be afraid of almost anything if you want to.

The most basic fear of all is the fear of fear, which itself generates and compounds fear by always delaying its acceptability. The other psychological fears are variants of this one; for, surprising as it may seem, psychological fears are not really about their objects. The objects are just an excuse to have a fear of fear. They act as the catalyst. Deep down, a person isn't really afraid of those things he or she is psychologically afraid of. It often happens that a person secretly *loves* those things or situations that apparently frighten them. Which is why those objects drew so much of their attention and energy to begin with.

We have nothing to fear but the fear of fear itself. So go ahead and feel it. After all, why shouldn't we want to feel fear—one of our own feelings—especially if there is no realistic danger involved? Why are we so obsessed with only feeling good or feeling safe? How can we ever hope to be complete human beings unless we feel our whole range of emotions? Why do we play favorites, preferring some emotions but avoiding others?

Pain

One answer is that society is generally biased against certain feelings and sends us many messages teaching us to avoid them. We have been trained. Take pain, the second of the emotional obstacles. Our lives are spent amid cultural signals telling us to fear, hate, and avoid pain.

Let's look at this a moment and determine the dynamics of the situation. The fear of pain is common. It is normal. Substances called *painkillers* are very popular and desirable. Much of medicine and psychotherapy (counseling) is aimed at alleviating or removing pain. Millions of people act dysfunctionally (drug abuse, violence, mental illness) in an effort to cope with their emotional pain. But could it be that almost everyone is wrong? Could all this be a bad case of "killing the messenger" on a mass level?

For pain—whether emotional or physical—is just that: a messenger. A signal that something is wrong and needs to be looked at and taken care of.

Suppose a wealthy man who lived in a mansion decided to install a state-of-the-art alarm system costing thousands of dollars to protect his home and family against burglary. And suppose that, one day, while he was relaxing in his study the alarm signal went off. But the man, finding the signal loud and unpleasant, decided to shut the system down, called the police and told them not to bother, and went back to listening to his music and drinking his glass of scotch. Most people would agree he acted foolishly. The alarm—which he took so much trouble and expense to install—was telling him of a possible problem that should be looked into. There could be an intruder on the premises. But, preferring not to deal with the unpleasant signal, he turned it off and declined to investigate its cause.

As absurd as the man in this example is, we all tend to do the same thing with pain. Nature has installed in us this most intelligent and effective signal to alert us to any inner problems (physical or emotional) so that we may address them, and the first thing we want to do is make it go away.

We could instead be celebrating each time we feel it. Not because we enjoy the pain as such, but because our alarm system is working. Whether due to hurt body or hurt feelings, it's telling us something needs to be checked out and healed. As if by magic, we're given a status report on ourselves. How unfortunate if we reject it. What if we loved it as our inner ally relaying a message to us?

When the source of pain is attended to and resolved, pain stops automatically. This is the only real and truly therapeutic "painkilling" there is. All others are temporary and cosmetic; of course, there is tremendous commercial interest in these latter "treatments" since they guarantee continued business by cleverly neglecting the causes of pain.

Guilt

The third of the major emotional obstacles, guilt, is also the subject of much confusion, and this cultural inheritance has helped sustain its power. Guilt has been incorporated into several of the prominent religious and spiritual belief systems and so has become associated with morality (the ethical judgment of whether things are good or bad). Unlike fear and pain, though, there is no natural counterpart to guilt. It is wholly psychological; that is, of the mind. With fear, there is the survival benefit of realistic fear. With pain, there is the similar advantage of having an accurate inner bodily signal. But guilt is completely created by thought. It's a human invention. Hence, the biblical story of Adam and Eve feeling ashamed upon acquiring the ability to make judgments ("eating from the Tree of Knowledge of Good and Evil"). While they had lived at the level of animals—naked and innocent—they could have no thought, shame, or original sin.

There is, however, a healthy counterpart to guilt, though it's also a mental creation: *remorse*. When feeling remorse, you realize you did something wrong, regret it, and vow never to do it again. You try to make amends and repair any damage your action caused; having accomplished these conditions, you move on. You learned from the experience and can let it go. This is the active aspect at work.

Guilt is quite different; it's the twisted version of remorse. As an emotional obstacle, it's designed to resist resolution. The person feeling guilty beats him- or herself up, sometimes even condemning him- or herself as being no good, a sinner, or beyond forgiveness. It may not matter that he's learned his lesson and apologized or made amends: he is guilty and no payment can atone for his infraction. It's very heightened drama. Absolution is resisted, for otherwise no more attention—from himself or others—could be called to his status as a wrongdoer. Like self-pity (which has a similar dynamic) or paranoia (a mental obstacle), guilt is the egotistic personality in disguise battling for recognition.

(There's also the emotional obstacle of pride, which is in the nature of inverted guilt. Here, the person has assumed the other side of morality and feels lofty, superior, judgmental, empowered, and so on, for having conquered or resisted sin. In mythology, it's depicted as the sin of Lucifer, who made a bid to take over heaven because he judged he was more good and more beautiful than God.)

The simplest and soundest course for managing guilt is to acknowledge and experience it, and let it change into remorse. You achieve this by opening to your active aspect while dealing with the issue.

The key to handling emotional obstacles is that fearing or rejecting them is the true obstacle. The emotions themselves are doorways. When the rejection is replaced with respect, we notice that the doors which seemed like locked barriers were really unlocked and all we needed to do was turn the knob.

Chapter 8
Understanding the Behavioral Obstacles

In Chapter 2, behaviors were described as actions performed with the body. These actions are often an outward indicator of the mind's thoughts and mind-body's emotions. Behaviors, judiciously worked, can have a healing and liberating effect. Intellectual understanding and emotional desire are in some respects just a preparation for taking action: for doing what you need to do.

The Meaning of Behavior

In psychology circles, there is sometimes disagreement on which of the three components (thoughts, feelings, behaviors) causes, or leads, the other two. Most everyone agrees they are correlated; the question is from which point. Experience and observation show that all three are interrelated, each one influencing and being influenced by the other two. Whenever one changes, there are responsive changes in the other two. If you're not sure of this, try a new *behavior* and see how you *think* and *feel* about it and about yourself. Or contact some repressed *feeling*, and afterward note what you *think* and how it has influenced your ability to *act*. Or *ponder* an important life issue with new information and a different perspective and note to what extent this influences your *emotions* and daily *behavior*.

The three components relate to one another via *meaning*, and meaning is a property of thought; the very interrelation is due to the fact that all three components are simply different expressions of the mind. (The body itself can be understood as a personification of the conscious/unconscious mind; in effect, the exterior aspect, or result, of the mind's work. Science agrees that the body is administered by the nervous system.)

Because feelings and behaviors aren't rational on their own, they arise or subside only in response to the meanings produced by thinking. Let's say you try a new behavior and it then influences your thoughts and emotions; regardless, you had to first *think* of it and decide to try it. But let's suppose the opportunity to try this behavior comes up spontaneously, without forethought; you try it and, as expected, it affects your thoughts and emotions. Yet still, the *behavior* went through a filter of meaning (as it were) to affect the other two components; without this meaning, it couldn't have any influence. The reason is that once you've learned language, every phenomenon you experience is endowed with word meaning. And if something is puzzling or nonsensical and appears meaningless, *that* becomes its meaning (i.e., "It means nothing to me," "I don't get it," etc.).

Occasionally it's speculated that emotion and behavior can occur in the absence of thought. But this could only apply to beings who haven't yet acquired language; once you know language, there's no turning back. You can not—under normal healthy circumstances—forget how to think or pretend you never thought. It's like birth: once you're born, you can't return to the womb. Certainly, you can transcend thought but that requires first having an active thought life: the difference between being pre-rational and post-rational. In any case, even after transcending thought, the personality continues using it for practical purposes.

While rational in structure, thoughts nevertheless have no consciousness or intelligence of their own—they are just products of the mind made to translate reality. Reality becomes mentality, which is more understandable by the conditioned mind. The mind itself is a more culturally acknowledged expression of the will, or the intelligent and aware will as it operates under the limits of reason and the five senses (and the body generally).

Avoidance and Habit

More than anything, personal progress is experiential: it's something you live. It thus makes perfect sense that the two main behavioral obstacles—*avoidance* and *habit*—prevent growth by limiting your experience.

Avoidance consists of not doing things that are learning or healing experiences—this includes not facing certain situations, people, or events; not approaching certain places or circumstances; and not engaging in certain activities. It does *not* include the avoidance of danger or disease. Habit consists of doing things automatically or routinely, over a period of time, to the point that they no longer promote learning or healing.

Usually, avoidance and habit work hand-in-hand to prevent self-development. The passive-reactive aspect here distorts your *doing* function; it maintains stagnation by having you not do what needs to be done (avoidance) and by having you do what should no longer be done (habit).

The antidote for avoidance is *approach*. Once you've determined that x action is worthy of your doing, proceed. Like Nike™ says, "Just do it." You've decided the action is for you. It's legal and safe. Go forward!

It may help to consider that, in the long run, it's much easier to do something necessary than to spend years refraining from doing it. The most difficult period is the one leading up to the impending act, when the mind tends to volley back and forth with anxiety and indecision ("Should I or shouldn't I?"), waging the civil war called "self-doubt." The word *doubt* has the same root as *double,* which is *duo* (two in Latin), indicating the mind is divided against itself, making it about half as useful as normal.

The antidote for habit is *substitution*. Pick an unimportant activity you always do and—instead—do something new or different that you know is right for you. Jump out of your rut.

Your habits can only be broken by breaking them. The responsibility is yours. People usually don't like the word *responsibility* applied to them, especially if they aren't doing well or could be doing better; they might think being responsible for their situation means it's their *fault*. Yet it isn't a matter of fault (which is similar to guilt), but simply responsibility. If you're not responsible for your failure, then you're not responsible for your success. You are powerful enough to psychologically ruin your life or enhance it. As a human being, you have this ability to steer your course and determine who you are. But if you don't take responsibility for it, how can someone else determine who you are for you?

Overcoming behavioral obstacles can be more powerful and effective than overcoming mental or emotional obstacles. Behaviors are enacted with the body and this physicality makes their accomplishment the most tangible and genuine—and least theoretical—of the three. Through action, they actualize. They're the "Put up or shut up" and "Walking the walk" of psychological development. Often, the direct experiences they provide are a necessary jolt, bringing allied improvements in thinking and feeling that would have taken much longer solely working the mental and emotional components.

Maybe it's because, as Shakespeare said, "All the world's a stage, and all the men and women merely players," and we can thus go out and really play. Have fun approaching the avoided and substituting the habitual.

To do or not to do? That is the question. To do *and* not to do. That is the answer.

An Interlude of Issues

Chapter 9
Relationships

Whether you're dating Raquel Welch, working out an armaments contract with Adolf Hitler, boxing Jake LaMotta, or playing lead guitar in KISS, you are in a relationship. You are relating to another or others: he, she or they is relating to you. I'm taking the stance that a relationship is made up of two people who interact with one another, whether in the briefest and most incidental encounter or the deepest and most lasting of bonds. There are many types of relationship: biological, marital, professional, romantic, friendly, adversarial, casual, spontaneous, and more. While these types rightly suggest a broad range of possibilities, they boil down to one constant: you and someone else in relation to one another.

It doesn't take a great genius with x-ray vision to realize that something is wrong with many of the relationships on the planet. A quick look at the evening news or flipping through a few pages of any history book will confirm the prevalence of abuse and violence within the human condition. While such conflict will always exist to some degree, it could be reduced if more people practiced a basic strategy designed to—at the very least—not feed into the cycles of unease and hostility.

It's notable that, in many relationships, discord is often preceded by *passivity* and/or *aggression*. In different (indeed, complementary) ways, each one leads the way to strife. Passivity invites conflict, aggression embodies it. Luckily, there's a third option that is harmonious and even: *assertiveness*. Of the three relating styles, assertiveness is the one that can be considered healthy; it's the social expression of the active aspect, while aggression and passivity are distinctly passive-reactive.

The aggressive person is inconsiderate of others' rights and feelings. Through words, actions, or both, he or she intimidates, coerces, and hurts. His needs are more important to him than others' needs. His anger is turned outward and manifests as *aggression*.

The passive person is overly considerate of others' rights and feelings, especially those of aggressive persons, and is quick to surrender his or her own rights when pressured. He isn't sufficiently protective of his own well-being and dignity. His anger is turned inward and manifests as *depression*.

The assertive person is considerate of his or her rights and feelings as well as those of others. His needs are important and he will pursue them, but not at someone else's expense. Others' needs may be important to him but he won't support them under intimidation or coercion. His anger is turned outward and manifests as *expression.*

Strategically, the stance of an aggressor is offensive, that of a passive person is defensive, and that of an assertive person inoffensive or counter-offensive (depending on what's most appropriate).

The aggressor empowers himself by disempowering others, and the passive person disempowers himself by empowering others at his expense—both approaches being recipes for unfairness and conflict. On the other hand, the assertive person empowers himself by not disempowering others and at times even by empowering them. He sticks up for himself but doesn't put others down unduly; she is direct in her speech and demeanor but not to the extent of being cruel or cutting. For these reasons, assertive conflict is fair and can lead to growth.

Assertiveness strikes the right balance. Neither too harsh nor too meek, it's the Golden Mean of human interaction. One is reminded of the scene where Goldilocks is in the Three Bears' home: "This bed is too hard [aggression]. This bed is too soft [passivity]. But this bed is *just right* [assertiveness]."

Aggressive and passive people both have a poor sense of boundaries. The aggressor intrudes upon others, the passive person permits others to intrude upon him. It's the assertive person that sets limits—both upon himself and others—so he won't violate others' boundaries or permit others to violate his.

Aggressors often have many interpersonal and allied problems: no one likes a bully or maniac. They often lose their temper and get into fights or break things; they can get into trouble with the law. Prisons are full of aggressors. Sometimes they are victims of people who fight back or get revenge on them for prior infractions.

Passive people also have many problems. They are taken advantage of and sometimes abused; their self-esteem is very low. They tend to give their belongings to aggressors. They often feel depressed, sometimes to the point of clinical Major Depression.

Assertive people can have interpersonal and allied problems, just like anyone else. However, most of these problems aren't a function of their own assertion but of having to deal with the aggressive and passive people who cross their path. Of the three styles, it's the least problematic in the long run and more ably manages any conflicts that do arise. But why is this the case? For one thing, aggressive and passive people usually attract one another; each's style finds completion in the other. But neither has much use for an assertive person. To an aggressor, an assertive person requires too much work and doesn't respond as he or she would like; to a passive person, someone who is assertive won't play into their disempowered role. The assertive type tends to deflect the other two by not reinforcing their strategies or meeting their needs. Sometimes he even brings out their positive qualities since their negative ones aren't being stimulated.

In summary, assertiveness by nature tends toward inner and interpersonal accord. With its built-in sense of ethics, moderation and confidence, others can be inspired to respond similarly. You may embody it in all your relationships, from the most intimate to the most incidental.

Chapter 10
Addiction

Addiction is an activity favored by the passive-reactive aspect to help prevent emotional healing. It's a problem that contributes to widespread unhappiness and so calls for more understanding. As usual, the relevant factors are fewer and simpler than the typical discourse suggests. The most workable ideas often tend to be simple: it's the restless intellect that likes to complicate things.

The first step is to assess what addiction is. There are various classes of addiction, including mental and emotional ones, but let's begin by looking at physical drug addiction, which is probably the most well-known.

The Body's Role

While addiction is a form of *dependence,* not all

dependence is addiction. Dependence at times is natural and necessary, while addiction never is. The body depends on substances such as air, water, and food; if these aren't ingested, the body signals its distress through gasping, thirst, and hunger, respectively. The more vital a substance, the more immediate and intense the distress signal: a person without food may subsist for many days during the gradual breakdown of the body; one lacking water might endure for many hours before thirst begins to take its toll; and someone deprived of air will feel desperate within seconds and die in minutes. This natural dependence on certain substances—with its system of signals—is of basic value to the body's survival and integrity.

This is *not* the case with addiction because an addictive substance isn't necessary for the body's well-being. To the contrary, it's often damaging. But if this is so, why does the addict's body emit distress signals when deprived of the chosen substance? Why is there craving, desperation, discomfort, and pain; in short, all the signs of bodily dependence? The answer is that there *is* a dependence, but it's a false one. A substance is physically addictive precisely because—through its chemical properties—it fools the body into regarding it an organic necessity; consequently, when it's no longer taken, the body panics and begins mimicking its own distress signals, which manifest as withdrawal symptoms. Physical addiction means a person's body has developed a dependence on a substance that serves no natural survival purpose. By extension, this usually indicates the dependence isn't healthy.

Concerned addicts need a simple mechanism to eliminate addiction. From an exclusively physical view, the mechanism is straightforward. We know the addictive substance is of no real use to the body, and that the distressing withdrawal symptoms are thus a false alarm: loud and piercing perhaps, but not indicative of real danger should the substance *ultimately* be withdrawn. As the substance is gradually withheld, and the body begins remembering it can function even better without it, the dependence is reduced and eventually disappears. Withdrawal symptoms are the body's learning course, and when the lesson is learned, the course ends. (Note: the sudden or medically unsupervised withdrawal from certain substances, such as alcohol, may be dangerous. Always check with a physician to assess the specific withdrawal concerns associated with a particular substance. In some cases, professional detoxification is recommended.)

**The Mind's Role
(The Need for Mental Withdrawal)**

With bodily withdrawal accomplished, physical

addiction is over; but the addiction itself may not be totally eradicated yet because the mental aspect—which is more complicated—is really the preeminent factor. The mind responds less rotely than the body because, through thought, it has the luxury of personal choice, and choice can breed doubt. If the recovering "addict" doesn't settle for the simple positive force of his active aspect, his mental withdrawal may be littered with complications; lessons learned could be forgotten, distorted, or denied; or resisted and not learned at all.

No matter what the individual's background, emotional makeup or life situation is, there's one issue common to *all* addicts: a difficulty or unwillingness to face their reality without their addiction. The underlying provocation may be trauma, boredom, anxiety, loneliness, irritation, or any other distressing state. Regardless, an addict seeks solace by directing his attention away from it, and so chooses to modify mood or alter perception. The anxious wish to evade that part of his psyche is his defining drive; mental withdrawal is the opportunity to stop evading.

Just like physical withdrawal brings bodily discomfort and misery, mental withdrawal features its own agony: loss of the shield protecting the mind from the keenness of psychological clarity. Because the mind tends to be sophisticated in its use of defenses and rationalizations, such sheer simplicity at first alarms it. Under the sway of the passive-reactive aspect, it will likely resist this simplicity even if the body is "clean" of the substance. Since the addict's wish to self-evade predated, and led to, his physical dependence, it probably hasn't been overcome by bodily withdrawal; the latter is just a step in the right direction.

The question is then: How can an addict come to terms with the fear of his own avoided feelings and insecurities? An addict can't repress these inner qualities without repressing a substantial part of himself; little good would come of it. As discussed in earlier chapters, avoiding these states tends to increase their power. The distance between them and their conscious integration gives rise to a frightening emotional void; addiction tries to fill this void with an imitation filler to pad its daunting emptiness—but the irony is that this prevents any genuine and natural fullness from occurring. Fortunately, the natural tendency is for the void to get filled sooner or later, one way or another, like a basin left outdoors before the rainy season; all the addict needs to do is allow it to happen without interfering. This is the big secret of overcoming addiction: by declining to artificially fill the void, the void *inevitably fills itself.*

Once physical withdrawal is accomplished, you should literally do nothing further about your addiction; this stillness allows mental withdrawal to begin. When you're used to employing so much energy to satisfy urges of dependence and self-distraction, inertia becomes a great ally. You start learning that withdrawal requires much less work than addiction. You no longer have to locate or take a substance, or deal with the many burdens that come with it. You're simply being true to your natural state, which is not being addicted.

With mental withdrawal, "doing nothing further" means returning to the mind's inherent simplicity. The job itself is very sparse, consisting of grinning and bearing it, and is the mind's version of the body's withdrawal pangs: a course of boredom, nervousness, discomfort, hopelessness, and confusion. Performed with the attitude of the active aspect, it's easier. Still, you may question your very existence. You may question the meaning of it all. You may never be the same again. But all this suffering is a good sign, serving the function of psychological growing pains: the more you face and feel your emotional pain, the more substantial and permanent your gain. With the dependent and avoidant tendencies (accumulated through addiction) breaking up, the mind-body can at last access more of its feeling and thinking faculties.

What is perhaps most helpful before embarking on this challenging process is to have outgrown the addictive purpose. The addict may acknowledge the value addiction held for him but now understands it's no longer worthwhile, and willingly surrenders the need to "self-medicate." This is important. It's practically useless for someone to force themselves to give up something they're not ready to surrender. This chapter addresses the addicted person who no longer has anything to learn from addiction and feels ready to live without its support. Presumably, everything—including addiction—happens for a reason; and for someone to renounce addiction without being satisfied as to its futility is counterproductive. To such a person, physically withdrawing from a substance has no bearing on her mental addiction: she may remain haunted by the substance's spectre and every day is then an obsessive walk across the tightrope of abstinence. She remains addicted in her thoughts and continues nurturing the void.

Besides Drugs

Because the mind doesn't need chemicals or drugs to be addicted, there are addictions that have nothing to do with substances. While behavioral addictions like gambling or emotional ones such as co-dependence are fairly well known, many others are less sensational and haven't necessarily been labeled "addictions" (e.g., nail-biting). Addiction can be viewed as any pattern of unnecessary thoughts, feelings, or behaviors—that distract, entertain or calm the self—on which someone relies to deter the awareness and integration of underlying (usually feared) ideas and emotions.

Thus, it can take a myriad of forms and almost everyone has a "habit" of one type or another. People often seek security in their personality patterns and may spend years displaying the same reflexive responses and prepared ideas and speech, especially when facing what could be challenging or novel situations. Or their lifestyles may feature various deeply-ingrained routines. Whether they're used to going to the beach, brothel, or bookstore, the habit can still be overcome by "doing nothing"—withdrawing from the activity and then *allowing* for the inevitable uncomfortable emptiness that opens up to be filled of its own accord.

Language's Role

There are problems with calling substance addiction a disease. It's definitely unhealthy, and may even be a disease when considered as *dis-ease* (not having ease or harmony) but not necessarily in the medical sense. The notion that substance addiction is a disease was likely an early act of political correctness, designed to help addicts feel more legitimized and less guilty. Yet it can also rob them of some personal power by implying that the "sick patient" has little or no responsibility for his condition; instead, he is a passive recipient of this bug, this infection, this *disease*. And yet, with substance addiction, the "disease" is always totally the product of the person's choices and actions.

While I believe Alcoholics Anonymous (AA) and Narcotics Anonymous (NA) have their merits and help many people, I have a concern with how they use language in some of their core concepts and interventions. Aside from considering addiction a disease, they ask every participant to state, "I am an alcoholic" or "I am an addict," with the intention of having him admit he has a problem. This is a case of language's power being misused and contributing to the perpetuation of a problem it's striving to solve. The statements establish identification with the condition. "I *am* an alcoholic." "I *am* an addict." Why would someone want to identify with something negative and unhealthy? If they want to acknowledge their problem, they can state it factually: for example, "I engage in addictive behaviors" or "I have been compulsively drinking alcohol." Note how these statements only report what's been experienced or done, and are free of self-labeling.

AA and NA participants are further taught to believe they'll "always" be alcoholics or addicts. This too is misleading and self-fulfilling. Only believing it can make it so. An addiction results from repeatedly engaging in particular patterns of thoughts, feelings, and behaviors; if those are resolved and disengaged, the person is no longer addicted. It's that simple. If she ever resumes those behaviors, feelings, and thoughts then she will—by definition—be demonstrating addictive traits at that time, but not a minute before. Someone who has fully resolved their alcoholism issues can drink occasionally or moderately, if they so choose: the difference between use and abuse. If they are physiologically allergic to alcohol, it's in their interest to avoid it as they would any other allergen.

Desire's Role

The role of desire in addiction has been minimized. Generally, people do what they want—sometimes even if it's not good for them. If it's unhealthy but *feels* good, they may do it anyway.

Ultimately, why do people do drugs? Because they *want* to. Why do people overeat? Because they *want* to. Let's just admit it, once and for all. When was the last time you had to really control yourself so that you wouldn't eat a bucket of dog shit? Or when did you last anxiously think to yourself, "Lord, I hope I don't see any dog shit on the streets today so I won't be tempted to eat it"? I didn't think so. See how easy it is to not do things when you don't want to?

Overcoming addiction is largely about trading desires. When the desire to desperately feel good right now *at any cost* gives way to your desire to feel good through balanced and active living, you can really progress.

The hardest part is at the beginning, when making the shift. But time is your ally. As you persist in your new attitudes, actions and choices, they become easier as your mind-body learns to work with them and discovers new comfort zones in health.

Chapter 11
Neurosis and Psychosis

There's an old saying, "Neurotics build castles in the air; psychotics live in them," that rightly indicates how the difference between the two is a matter of degree. Neurosis stiffens the personality with unresolved fear, pain or guilt complexes; psychosis takes these complexes to their conclusion. While there's considerable waste of personal energy in neurosis, the use of energy during psychosis is impaired to the point that psychological fragmentation and self-defeat prevail outright. Psychosis, then, may be said to represent passive-reactivity in its purest form.

Conscious or Unconscious Mind?

Psychological functioning occurs along a continuum

of degrees indicating the extent of emotional harmony, as follows:

1. Least harmony: psychosis
2. Slight harmony: neurosis
3. Average harmony: normality
4. Increased harmony: active aspect
5. Most harmony: superconsciousness (will)

The more neurotic a person's functioning, the more problematic their relationship with reality; when it reaches the point of psychosis, there's an overload of the cognitive structure. This breakdown occurs along the boundary between the conscious and unconscious minds so that the separation between them is no longer clear, and compromises both of the conscious mind's key functions, *thinking* and *sensing*.

We covered thinking in earlier chapters. Sensing is the mind taking data received through the five senses and organizing it into a coherent perceptual field, enabling you to accurately make your way through the world. Sensing and thinking work together, with thought using language to classify and make meaning of the sensory data.

The unconscious mind's key function is *imagining*, which is similar to the conscious mind's *sensing* function—it can imagine sights, sounds, tastes, smells, and touches—with the difference that its sensory material doesn't come through the body's five senses but is created in the unconscious itself out of information it perceives and/or generates. In dreams, for instance, you find all your senses intact: you can see things, touch things, listen, smell, and so on*. But meanwhile your physical body is laying in bed asleep with its eyes closed. You may be visiting the most faraway and strange places, and yet your body hasn't gone anywhere. How could this be? Your unconscious mind-body is getting energy and translating it into scenes, sounds, and sensations. When awake, your conscious mind-body does the same exact thing, but with energy received by the five senses.

Because our personality revolves around the physical body, it usually supposes that the conscious mind's information is "more real" than the unconscious mind's. But it's not that it's more or less real; it simply has a different sphere of activity. While dreams might appear unreal upon awakening, they appear real enough when we're in them. Similarly, our awake world may appear unreal looked at from the viewpoint of the dream state.

In psychosis, there is dysfunctional blending of the two spheres—material from the unconscious imagination seeps into the conscious mind. When thinking is

---

*This applies especially to lucid dreams; but in ordinary dreams, most people find that seeing and hearing are the most emphatic senses.

compromised, the result is *delusion;* when sensing is compromised, *hallucination.* With this incoherent spilling over of unconscious material, the conscious mind doesn't operate in a normative manner; neither thinking nor sensing is harmonious or indicative of socially shared reality.

Normally, you can think any bizarre thought ("My neighbor is an intergalactic spy from Orion" or "Archie will feel jealous if I have a threesome with Betty and Veronica") or imagine any unrealistic sensory scene (a green sky and blue grass with a red ocean) and know it's only a product of your imagination. The boundary between conscious and unconscious is clear; and each is doing what it's supposed to. But to the person experiencing psychosis, where the two spheres overlap, the thoughts he *imagines* seem reasonable and true, and the sense perceptions he *imagines* seem tangible and externally real. (Although visual and auditory hallucinations are the most common, all five senses can be affected by psychosis; there are also olfactory (smell), gustatory (taste), and tactile (touch) hallucinations.)

Sometimes people ask, "Are spiritual visions and paranormal phenomena indicative of psychosis? Are mystics and psychics psychotic?" The answer is "No" because there are senses beyond the typical five which may be more developed in some persons than in others. This is not the same as the disorderly blending of the unconscious and conscious. Granted, reports of extrasensory perception may appear strange to a five-senses person. But this would be like landing in a country where all the natives are blind (having only the other four senses). Their society would naturally be arranged without consideration for visual phenomena, which they wouldn't understand or even know existed. And if you started talking about colors and all the sights you were seeing, they would think you were either mad or a liar.

End of Interlude

Chapter 12
Lifestyle

Now that we've covered thought, feeling, and behavior with the issues and obstacles each presents, we're more prepared to apply these concepts day to day. It's through application that knowledge becomes a lived experience: otherwise it stays theoretical. In this information age, we often assume that having knowledge is enough; but in fact it's the first step. And like any first step, it alone won't get you too far. Mainly, it prepares you to take the next step—trying out what you've learned.

Your progress in mind managing can be bolstered if you first consider that *everything in life is important and interesting and can teach you something.* If you, armed with this mantra, incorporate all phenomena (everything you think, feel, do, and perceive) into your development path, no experience is wasted. Adopting such a holistic attitude, it's easier to embrace events and situations that you may previously have thought irrelevant or disagreeable. Attention is key: the greater your drive to self-develop and the more effort you invest, the more life circumstances it includes.

The totality of how you live your life—what you do and how you do it, who you associate with, where you go, what you put in your body, what you think about, how you deal with problems—is what I refer to as your *lifestyle*. You integrate something into your lifestyle by accepting the role it can play in your progress. Diet? Check. Friends? Check. Cultural knowledge? Check. Mindset while driving through heavy traffic? Check. Emotional response to unpleasant co-worker? Check. And so on, down the line, every event beautifully valuable. Be open to what each situation tells you; for example, if something isn't going well it may be a sign you have something to learn in that area. Approaching life with this intent, you think of whatever is happening as a piece to the greater puzzle and try to determine how it fits and what it's giving you—since you're giving *it* attention. You can live each moment with this openness and focus.

Time Managing

The word "moment" is interesting. It generally refers to "a very brief unit of time." The word carries both the connotation of importance (momentous) and transience (momentary). It derives from the Latin *momentum,* meaning "movement." The derivation suggests time's relation to space since movement takes time, and needs space, to occur. So a moment is a space-time instant which has great import and yet is fleeting. A lot can happen in any given moment. The sum of all your moments makes up your life.

Every day brings its own supply of moments, and each moment is a new opportunity for choice: Should I carry on like this or strike out in a bold new direction? Do I take a positive, negative, or neutral stance? What's important right now? There's considerable power in these choices because a moment can be a seed for future developments, but how often do we value this and act upon it? The days tend to roll by like a blur, and we slosh along as if in a habitual trance. Life then seems generic and not especially momentous. Day in and day out, over and over: unless we do something "special." Then we're okay with that day because we've been entertained. But what if each day was seen as essential? Take April 7, 1998. Never before that day in the history of the universe was it ever April 7, 1998; nor, after, will it ever be again. It's completely unique. On that day, everything which occurred will never occur that way again, just like it never occurred that way before. It serves as a special link in the long history of time. This goes for every day. You can break it down further and say each hour of every day is unique. Break it down even more: to each minute, each second. Each moment totally unique, never to be repeated.

Energy Managing

Ever notice that people who do little are often tired, while those who do a lot tend to be energized? You may think inactivity is restful and that keeping busy is exhausting. To an extent, it's true. But, beyond that, it can get to the point where the less you do the harder it is to do anything, and the more you do the easier it is.

Sarah Bernhardt once said, "Energy creates energy." On the other hand, physicists assert that "energy can neither be created nor destroyed." So which is it? If energy can't be created, it can certainly be generated. And it takes energy to generate more energy since *to generate* is a verb. The implication is that, for you to be energized, at some point you have to get moving.

If you were to spend three months laying in bed, you'd find that what had always been one of the easiest activities—standing up and taking a couple steps—would now be the most difficult challenge. You'd have almost no stamina, and your leg muscles would be atrophied and barely able to support your body weight. Walking to the bathroom and standing in front of the toilet would be an odyssey from which you may not make it back in one piece. Anything but laying in bed would feel exhausting.

On the other hand, to the active person, resting any more than necessary feels like being imprisoned. To just lay around as the thrill and excitement of life rush by is torture.

The balanced stance is to be active but know how to rest; energized but not frenetic, calm but not lazy. This middle path produces a state of willingness and enthusiasm, combined with patience and steady attention.

Habit Managing

In day to day life, harnessing the cumulative power of *habit*, without being a slave to it, is useful. You become skilled at those things you do over and over; if you then keep doing them even more, you'll eventually be an expert at them. Each of us is an expert at different things, not all of them positive. Some of us are experts at complaining and having low self-esteem, others at being nervous, yet others at doing drugs or smoking cigarettes.

Have you ever seen novice smokers? They don't even inhale the smoke but just blow it out their mouths. When they do inhale, they gag and cough and their eyes tear. Complete amateurs. But if they keep at it, soon they're able to smoke correctly. If they keep at it even longer, they eventually graduate to grandmaster smoker and can smoke a whole cigarette by inhaling it in three or four drawn-out puffs, leaving an impossibly long ash hanging on till it's flicked just so. They can blow smoke rings and French inhale, and forty cigarettes a day feel nice.

Pick your habits wisely because once you do something enough times, it will become so easy that it'll almost appear to do itself. You'll be an expert at it whether you like it or not.

Dropping an old habit is so hard because every time you engaged in it, you fed it. A habit is like a wild beast—the more you feed it, the stronger it gets. If you want to kill it, starve it. And just like a beast, when you first starve it, it'll kick up its heels and rant and rave and try to tear up the place. But if you persist and keep starving it, soon it will start weakening and eventually die.

Building up new habits also takes persistence; you have to keep feeding them until they get strong. Unfortunately, many of us want to start something new and master it right away, and when that doesn't happen we give it up. We forget that everything we do well, that seems natural and easy, is an acquired skill that once took lots of effort. The easiest things—walking, talking, reading, writing, tying your shoelaces, driving a car—were at first difficult and awkward. At the time, we doubted we'd ever master them. They took months, or even years, of practice. We probably would've given up if someone (a parent, older sibling, or teacher) hadn't made us continue. If you look at a young child learning to walk, you see the uncertainty: each step is shaky and has to be coordinated with the next. Alternating the left foot with the right causes confusion and strain. Then the child falls. But his caretaker ensures he doesn't stop trying and soon he's practicing again. After a few months, he's running about with nary a thought.

As grown-ups, we don't have a caretaker to keep us from quitting so it's up to us to make sure we pick ourselves up and keep moving along.

The next chapter presents a series of practices that can help develop the attention, understanding, and direction so vital for stimulating progress.

Chapter 13
Practices

1. Wordless Thought

Practice thinking without words. At first, this may seem paradoxical. But what you'll be doing is considering only the momentary ideas that usually lead right to word thoughts. An idea or the knowledge of something takes an instant. It's the thinking it out in words that takes time and this is what you *won't* be doing in this exercise.

Pay attention to your mind's activity with an attitude of readiness. When you have an idea, at that instant move on to something else—refrain from translating it into language in your mind. This is much easier than always having to come up with words. Settle for the cognition that pre-exists the wordy ideas you normally have. With more practice, you'll notice you understand things even better by not needing to mentally translate them into word format.

Benefits: Helps you save time and conserve mind-body energy.

2. Facts vs. Judgments

Pay close attention to every statement you think, say, hear, or read; and each time ask yourself, *"Is that a fact or judgment?"* Be aware that judgments are often stated as facts (e.g., "Picasso's work is a joke" vs. "I think Picasso's work is a joke"). You'll need to see through the false grammar. If a statement is a fact, let it be. If it's a judgment, assess whether it's an opinion or belief (opinions pertain to evident things, beliefs to phenomena not evident to the senses). Note whether the judgment is positive (favorable) or negative (unfavorable).

Consider many of your cherished ideas and those of family, friends, and culture. Are they factual or judgmental? Is a statement true (factual) just because it's positive or earnestly believed?

Benefits: Makes these two types of thought more distinct. Helps you notice how people often blend them, resulting in confused perceptions or faulty expectations (such as giving assumptions and beliefs the weight of evidence).

3. Vigilant Refraining

Mind managing is a question of doing what's healthy

but also of not doing what's unhealthy. What we don't do and exclude is just as pivotal as what we do and include. Sometimes even more so. Not drinking cyanide is more important for my health than drinking carrot juice.

To do this practice, choose an unhealthy class of statement that's habitual for you. If you often think or say statements that maintain traits such as low self-esteem, pessimism, jealousy, selfishness, or impatience, choose accordingly. Then make a vow to not think or say this type of statement for one week. For instance, declare, "I vow that, for the next seven days, I will think no thoughts and utter no statements that put me down in any way." Or, as another example, "For the next seven days, I won't think any pessimistic thoughts about my future." Keep a steady vigilance and stay aware, noting every time you break the vow. (If you want, keep a little log, making a mark for each break and noting how many breaks a day occur.) At the end of the seven days, you can renew the vow or choose another type of thought to refrain from.

Benefits: Improves your ability to disengage from old mental habits, and helps you realize you have options.

4. Literal Meaning

Interpret literally each statement you hear or read, appreciating it through the concrete definition of the words. If someone says, "I feel blue," consider blue as the color. If you read a quote such as "I like heavy metal," wonder whether they mean lead or steel. If someone politely asks, "How do you do?" respond, "How do I do what?" If someone shouts, "Holy shit!" reflect on how feces is indeed sacred since it results from the maintenance of an organism's life energy and also fertilizes the earth.

Benefits: Helps you understand the relative absurdity and falsity inherent in language, and how the meanings we have given to words are ultimately arbitrary, as are the words themselves. Language can then be taken less seriously.

5. Feeling Fully

To begin this exercise, be receptive of the opportunities—that will inevitably arise—to feel emotionally hurt. Everyday living provides many circumstances in which our emotional hurts can come out to be exposed and released. If we let it happen, we can feel to heal.

Normally, our passive-reactive aspect induces us to dislike and reject these hurts, which keeps them hidden and trapped inside us. Rejecting one of our inner hurt feelings doesn't mean it will go away but that it won't come out. If we didn't have these unhealed hurts inside us in the first place, we would be better positioned, and more eager, to manage distressing and potentially painful events. Inner hurts act as emotional sore spots that increase our vulnerability.

In this exercise we're out to do the opposite of what is "normal." We open up to feeling our emotional hurts and owning them. We listen closely for our passive-reactive signals. The signals usually begin with a stirring of emotional discomfort: suddenly, because of what someone said, or a look they gave you, or some unpleasant news you heard, or some difficult event that's occurring, or some negative idea you thought of, you begin to feel nervous. Or maybe insecure, sad, frightened or plagued by self-doubt.

So far, so good. Now maintain your presence, and recognize you are more than any feeling you have. Locate the feeling: where is it, exactly? In your chest, neck, head, abdomen, or back? Or is it throughout your body? Once you locate it, allow yourself to experience it some more. Then discover its meaning. Behind each hurt feeling, there's a meaning; sometimes it's many years old and you might be surprised to find some old belief or assumption that gave it power. When you sense you've encountered the meaning, summarize it in one key sentence; this will be the whole gist of the feeling for you. It could be something like "I am stupid" or "I'm scared of dying" or "People hate me," and so on.

Once you have the key sentence, be with it, consider it; allow it to float around you and through you; say it aloud or in your mind and listen openly to it, all the while permitting yourself to contact the feelings and reactions your mind-body is making. Now examine how real this sentence has been for you; the degree of truth it has or that you assumed it has. Spend as much time with it as you think necessary; it could be a few minutes, an hour or two, or more.

This exercise goes contrary to the normal act of suppression. Instead of avoiding or denying hurt feelings, you open to them and feel them through. In effect, you tell your mind-body, "It's okay. I'm working with you, and I'm ready to take these things of mine that I used to consider threats."

Closely experiencing the key sentence proves to your mind that you're no longer shying away from the threat and neutralizes the meaning's heavy charge, reducing or taking away its sting.

Benefits: Promotes emotional healing by engaging, understanding and releasing your old hurt feelings.

6. Approach to Fear

Pick one of your psychological fears; something which frightens you but that you know isn't truly dangerous to your physical well-being—it could be a situation, person, thing, or place. Make the necessary arrangements to approach it. For instance, if you're afraid of speaking in public, join Toastmasters or volunteer to speak in public somewhere. If you're afraid of being rejected by a woman, ask a woman out. If you're afraid of being seen as different or unconventional, spend a few hours walking around town dressed in a strange costume of your own design.

You may have certain ideas about what might constitute failure at this exercise. Don't strive to avoid those failure outcomes; to the contrary, hold failure as a glory in its own right, on a par with success. Anyone can feel happy with success, but feeling happy with failure requires a special strength of spirit. If you want to assess someone's character, observe whether they deal graciously with losing, not with winning. Try hard to fail. Why not? Or at least realize that to fail is to succeed at having gone through an experience.

The goal is not to win or lose, conquer or be conquered: it is to *experience*. If you go through with what you fear, you're doing well. It takes courage to experience fear. The only way to *truly* lose here is by avoiding the task. To approach and experience is victory; to shun and avoid is defeat. That's all. If you ask a woman out and she responds, "Get lost, dork," you win. Because you did what you feared and she can't take that away from you. Her response is irrelevant. If she responded, "Yes, I'd love to," that wouldn't make the exercise more successful (no matter how much you personally prefer this outcome).

When you approach that fearful something,

experience actively what it's like to be there. Give yourself permission to really live the moment. You're the only one who's truly authorized to give you that license. Focus on what your senses are giving you: what do you see, hear, smell, taste, and touch during the experience? Realize it's an honor to receive that information. Whether it feels fun or highly uncomfortable makes no difference; just live it fully, warts and all. It's a way to tell your mind, "I can take it. And I do take it."

After, acknowledge that you approached a fear and enlarged your behavioral repertoire. Be aware your mind will likely start forming judgments (favorable or unfavorable) about the experience. When this happens, know it's a response that is not necessarily important and certainly not factual.

A few days later, you can try the exercise with another psychological fear.

Benefits: Helps you find out how things that were frightening when continuously avoided lose much of their fearsomeness upon approach. The mystery and power that ruled from afar don't impress the same when seen close up.

7. Habit Substitution

Each of us is bound by habits: routine activities that are part of our daily schedules, indeed often make up the very patterns of our lives. Some may have been repeated so often and are so woven into our lifestyles that they've taken on a certain magnitude. These habits can even shape our identities; they're so normal to us that they appear fundamental to who we are as people. But are they? A life habit usually doesn't start as a habit but becomes one through a recurrence that isn't checked. There may initially be a valid reason for this recurrence; maybe the repeated activity is a good defense mechanism and lowers anxiety. The automatic repetition of habits can provide stability and dependability. Yet this can go overboard, resulting in stagnation and rigidity. When that happens, it means you've outgrown the habit but are still dragging it around with you out of . . . habit.

In life, you can't do everything; while you spend time and energy doing *this,* you can't do *that.* If you keep doing *this* more than you need to, and continue with it, but doing *that* is what will help you grow, then doing *this* is keeping you down. In the physical universe, there's an interaction between stability and change, between constants and variables. Matter exists (stability) but at the same time is constantly, though sometimes very subtly, being transformed (change) through aging or other modifications. In the psychological sphere, people likewise do best when they embody both these principles. There are times to hang on and times to let go.

A habit that is initially healthy can, with time or overuse, become unhealthy. Then it's time to let go. The present practice teaches you to release the old and reach for the new—whether or not the new becomes a habit will be up to you and your needs.

Select one of your typical habits—it could be the midnight snack, watching TV, reading, hanging out at the mall, biting your fingernails, or saying "you bet"— one that isn't necessary for your health or livelihood. (You can either pick a negative habit with a view to not resuming it, or a positive one you'll resume afterward. The point of the exercise is to learn you are more than any of your habits and can experience life without it.) Then select an activity that isn't habitual for you—it could be eating a different type of food, engaging in a new behavior, going to a type of place you normally wouldn't frequent, and so forth. For fourteen days, refrain from doing the habitual one and instead do the new one. Let's suppose you normally play video games five hours a day but have never tried Japanese food; in this exercise, you wouldn't play video games for fourteen days but during that period have Japanese food, say, four times.

For the new activity, it's good to pick something you think normally "doesn't go" with your self-image. The more different, the better. Extra points if it feels potentially discomfiting and awkward. If you're a casual "beach bum" or "slacker" type, buy a suit and tie with dress shoes and wear them to a restaurant or party (and stop skateboarding). If you're the bookwormish indoor type, go kayaking or jogging (and stop reading). And so on. These "types" are usually just identities resulting from habit complexes. The idea is to broaden your range and overcome your prejudices about yourself and what you like and supposedly don't like. Try to see how the "other half" lives. Do something you always thought was "dumb" or "useless." You might surprise yourself. Not liking things often results from not understanding them.

Benefits: Expands your personal horizons and energizes your capacity to choose your habits instead of having them choose *you*.

8. Meditation

Meditation is a word that can mean different things because it encompasses various types and techniques, and also because it has several general definitions, ranging from "contemplation" to "concentration" to "yoga" to "mysticism." The common ground in all this is the phenomenon of directed consciousness: you have decided to pay attention to something that you don't typically attend to sufficiently. Through this act, you become better acquainted with it. For instance, if you really want to know about sunsets, you may decide to spend an hour every evening for one month silently watching the sun go down. When you do this, you're bound to directly notice things about the sunset that prior escaped your attention. Some of these things may have previously been noted by scientists or painters or poets; but, regardless, you are now perceiving them yourself. Because you paid enough attention.

And so it is with your mind. How conscious are you of its workings? How much attention do you pay to it really? You're very close to it and yet what you usually know is the surface: the conscious mind (i.e., the part of the mind you're conscious of). It's like being able to look at a watch and tell time but thinking that's all there is to a watch—having no idea about the works and gears or the battery and electronics inside.

What does the mind normally do? And when or in what circumstances? How does it make thoughts? And which types, and how often? What patterns are discernible? How do these thoughts give rise to feelings? Or is it the other way around? What *is* the mind, anyway? Where does consciousness start? Where does it end?

These are questions that mankind has been asking for centuries, and the answers are found by listening to your mind. There is no substitute for direct perception and experience. Mind managing is most successful when you know your mind. You need to be aware of what you're working with. This goes for everything, by the way. How can you manage your employees if you don't know who they are, where they work, or what they're supposed to do? How can you be a good auto mechanic if you don't know car engines and the tools needed for the job?

Knowledge of mind can't come solely from books or speeches because then you would just be taking an expert's word for it. What if he's wrong? Or lying? You need to know directly, for yourself. Then you don't need the experts.

There are two advantages to paying close attention to your mind: first, you become less of a stranger to yourself, getting better acquainted with the inner rhythms, workings, and movements of your mind-body; second, you begin to note that you and your mind aren't synonymous. It may dawn on you: "Wait a minute, if I'm paying attention *to* my mind then in some way I must be apart *from* my mind." Anything you can perceive with your senses or think about isn't you. It may be of you, but is not you yourself.

When you're ready to meditate, sit in a firm comfortable chair with your back straight. It's better for your back not to lean against the backrest. Your back should be straight during the entire exercise, not leaning or resting on anything. Place your hands, palm down, on your lap. Your knees should be bent at an angle of 90 degrees, with your feet flat on the ground, a few inches apart, pointing straight forward. Your head should also be held straight, with your eyes looking straight ahead. Hold the position perfectly still for 15 minutes; stay frozen like a statue. The only movements should be those of the chest and diaphragm due to breathing, and blinking of the eyes (the exercise can also be done with the eyes closed).

During the exercise, you will most likely feel an unbearable temptation to move in any number of ways: twitch, stretch, shift in your seat, sniff, clear your throat, scratch, nod, lick your lips, tap your fingers, and many more. Stay still. Let's say you develop an incredible desire to nod your head. Stay still. Let's suppose a mosquito lands on your cheek and you are dying to shoo it away. Stay still.

If you do move, just let it go and immediately resume your stillness. But the more you resist such temptations, the more you'll strengthen and discipline your energy and build up your control of the body.

By holding this position, you are straightening yourself out, rectifying body and mind, opening up and clarifying the flow of your energy. In yoga, the position is sometimes called "the king" or "the pharaoh"; there are numerous pictures of pharaohs sitting in this position in ancient Egyptian murals. Basically, this is the position your body really wants to sit in once it's fit enough; it creates the least amount of strain because it observes the body's lines and symmetry. If you're used to having bad posture, or walking crooked, or looking down a lot, this position will initially be especially uncomfortable. You will now be using muscles that are weak and easily fatigued because they've hardly ever been used. Look at this exercise as a workout in stillness. If you can, have a friend watch you so that every time you slip out of position he or she can give you feedback and gently help reposition you as necessary.

If you're like most people, at first you'll find the exercise unbearably uncomfortable, exhausting, and tedious. Uninformed observers often look at some expert doing this meditation and say, "That's it? My God, that's nothing. It looks so easy." All they see is someone sitting in a chair doing nothing. Until they try it. Then they have a newfound respect for it. The 15 minutes may appear like they'll never end. Each minute seems like five. You may perspire a lot. You may get pains in your muscles and bones (if they're not used to being straight). You may get very nervous and anxious. Note that these are all signs you're doing the exercise right. If you embark on this exercise and from the first session it feels easy, chances are you're doing it wrong: you are likely getting out of position in subtle degrees and unconsciously catching little rest breaks. While this definitely provides relief, it lessens the effectiveness of the practice. That's why it helps to have someone watch over you, giving you feedback and correcting the slip-ups in your position, until with enough practice you've trained your body to recognize the right posture and have sufficient stamina to stay in it for the needed time. (If you can't find someone to watch you, do it facing a fullview mirror.)

While you hold the position, breathe in and out through your nose, mouth closed. At the same time, pay attention to the ideas, notions, images, sensations, memories, and chatter your mind produces. Do so as a neutral witness. Instead of forming judgments about your mindstuff, do something even simpler: not form judgments. If you have a repulsive taboo thought, don't think, "How horrible!" If you have a brilliant idea, don't think, "Awesome!" In fact, don't think, period. Or, at most, form a fact: "That was a thought."

You are listening in on your own head. Self-eavesdropping. Let your mind run free and wild; or not. Whatever your mind does is appropriate since that is what your mind is doing. If you feel any pressure or discomfort or fatigue, it's likely your emotional energy is being unblocked and released. (That's a positive development, even if it doesn't feel good while it's happening; later, you'll be much more refreshed.) In general, listen to your mind as you would to a river flowing by. Don't worry about, or get excited by, the meanings it makes: just listen to what it produces as pure sound.

Once you can do the exercise easily for 15 minutes, increase to 30. Once that's easy, do 45. Progress will be more steady if you do it twice a day, ideally before breakfast and before dinner. It can also be done before bedtime, if at least two hours have elapsed since dinner.

Benefits: Stabilizes, strengthens, and refreshes the mind-body; increases direct knowledge of same. Aligns and harmonizes your energy.

9. Here Now

Presence consists of being open to the present, *as it is,* without weighing it down with recall or expectation. Being so absorbed in it that you are too centered and aware to think about it or other things. The moment you put your thinking cap on, you distract your attention away from what is.

My psychological problems are due to me letting my thoughts and feelings about the past or future burden me. Logically speaking, once a troublesome situation is over, it should no longer be a problem for me. And, prior to its occurrence, it also shouldn't be a problem. But that's usually not how it works because I'm probably spending a lot of time pondering what happened or what may happen. A problem is creatively woven together out of individual cognitive strands called "meanings" that are themselves creative products. Otherwise, how could something that literally doesn't exist (outside of my thought) be problematic?

A psychological problem is different from a concern. Concern indicates a responsible stance toward a realistic dilemma that is occurring or likely to occur. Having concern means you're working with the difficulty and striving to come up with an answer or resolution. It also indicates you care about the situation. A psychological problem, on the other hand, is *caused* and *maintained* by thinking.

In the here and now, there can be realistic problems but no psychological ones. If—in the present—you are being held up at gunpoint, then that's a realistic problem in so much as you are being robbed and may be shot. If you maintain a state of presence during that situation, you won't add psychological problems to it. You won't worsen your circumstances by thinking or saying or doing the wrong thing, or by being inappropriately passive either. If you maintain your presence, you'll automatically and intuitively take the most harmonious course of action or non-action indicated at that time and place. This course can't be predicted. Every person is different and so is each event; furthermore, each moment is unique and conditions change by the moment. There is no guarantee of a successful outcome, since you're not the only participant involved, but you will have done your part.

To live consciously in the present, it helps to realize that's all there is. In other words, you are living in the present. Right now. All the time. The now is literally eternal: it's always now. Physically, there is no past and future. You do not live in the past or future. You wouldn't be able to, no matter how hard you wanted to.

No one ever has or ever will. No matter how terrible last Tuesday was, it's over. And it's not coming back. Ever. The *past* and *future* are mental constructions we deal with in the *present* out of habit, for convenience and entertainment. But your body is always in the now; only your mind habitually ignores it. Living in the present is too simple for the mind to understand.

To do this exercise, spend ten minutes only attending to the present. If you're doing it with one or more other people, then it'll also entail speaking only about the present and only the present tense will be used. Only things that are part of the here and now can be thought of or discussed. If it's not here (in this setting) *and* now (at this time), it doesn't exist. What happened here last week or three seconds ago is irrelevant; same goes for what's happening now in the next town or across the street. You may think or talk about what your five senses perceive in and around you. If you see it, you may say, "I see the yellow letters on that poster," or if you feel it, you may say, "My foot is cramped." Each time a participant mentions something that isn't in the here and now, another one can say "here now" as a reminder. If you're doing it alone, it's best to simply let the infraction go because it's already "here now" again anyway. (Or, rather, it still is.)

Benefits: Helps you experience what it's like to focus on the present, and shows how much your attention is usually embedded in past-future thinking.

10. What Problem

This practice is useful when you feel overwhelmed by problems. Sit down comfortably and ask yourself, "What problems do I have right here and right now, sitting in this chair?" Then search for the answer. Find out which problems are affecting you at this very time and place. Once you identify them, probe each one further to make sure what you're dealing with is *really* problematic to you here and now.

I've used this exercise with clients to help them separate their realistic from their psychological problems and show them how the latter are just phantoms spun from their own thoughts. For example:

CLIENT: I have so many problems, it's driving me crazy. It's very depressing. I can't seem to deal with them.

ME: What problems do you have right here and right now?

CLIENT: Right here and right now?

ME: Yeah, right here and right now, sitting in that chair.

CLIENT: Well, I'm about to be evicted from my apartment.

ME: Right here and right now?

CLIENT: Uh . . . well, no. But this week, maybe tomorrow.

ME: Alright, that's a concern. And when you leave here you can begin to do something about it, like look for a new place to live. But, right now and here in that chair, what problems do you have?

CLIENT: My girlfriend and I fight a lot. She recently had an affair with someone.

ME: Okay. But are you and your girlfriend fighting right now in this office?

CLIENT: No. . . .

ME: Where is your girlfriend now?

CLIENT: She's at work.

ME: Is she having the affair right now?

CLIENT: It happened about two months ago.

ME: So how is this a problem to you here and now?

CLIENT: I'm pissed off and hurt about it here and now. I don't know if I can trust her ever again.

ME: You said, "I *am* pissed off and hurt about it." Is that who you *are?* Or is that what you feel?

CLIENT: Yeah, it's what I feel.

ME: Okay, you feel pissed off and hurt about it and mistrustful toward her.

CLIENT: Damn right.

ME: So these feelings are a problem?

CLIENT: Yeah.

ME: Fair enough. How are they a problem to you?

CLIENT: They don't feel good.

ME: And how is not feeling good a problem to you?

CLIENT: I prefer to feel good than bad.

ME: That's your preference?

CLIENT: Yeah.

ME: And how is not getting that preference a problem?

CLIENT: Uh . . . I don't know.

Doing this sort of analysis with problems can teach you that having problems is sometimes not a problem at all. Tracing your problem feelings to their root thoughts, and reaching the frontiers of reason, you may discover that the logic creating your problems isn't internally coherent. Problems are less impressive when their core falls apart under scrutiny. The pressure is off and it's uplifting to learn you have more leeway in handling them than you thought. You certainly have a *right* to be overwhelmed by any problem, if you so choose. It's understandable if you are. But you don't *have* to be, is the point.

As you practice questioning how problematic each problem really is for you at this time and place, it'll gradually become evident that the control you have over your psychological problems is great—since you're their author in the first place. This frees you up to work with whatever realistic problems you may have.

In a sense, all problems are psychological—something is problematic to us because we disapprove of it and its likely outcome. But, for the purpose of practical distinction, we term "realistic problems" those situations originating outside our minds which most people would reasonably be concerned over. If you ask someone if they have any problems here and now, and they respond, "Yes, I have cancer" or "I have a fresh snake bite on my arm," these are objective situations that imperil the body and aren't simply concocted by thoughts and feelings.

When you do the practice, if you find a realistic problem, remember that any judgments or feelings you have *about* it are psychological. Isolate, and pay mind to, the facts. But should you find psychological problems, do the exercise all the way through for each one separately. It's when you try to deal with many problems at once, or jump back and forth between them, that they seem overwhelming. This is unnecessary.

Benefits: Demonstrates how psychological problems are caused by mental activity about the past and future, and not by the past and future themselves (which can't touch you).

Chapter 14
Concluding Remarks

If instruction on how to heal yourself while enhancing your development could be conveyed in one word, it would be *feel*. For, as it is, most of our barriers are made up of that certain hardness which lodges itself in our psyche, out of fear and self-protection, and—perhaps with the best intention—prevents feeling from flourishing. This accounts for most subsequent psychological trouble.

Be in touch. Grasp it. Get a grip. Ground yourself. These are all "feeling" terms. They have physicality and suggest the body, without which you can not feel.

The trick is to feel in the right (i.e., active) way. How do you know you're feeling actively and it's not merely melodrama or wayward sentimentality? Easy: it has to be a learning experience. Unless learning takes place—a new viewpoint or understanding—it's likely just theatre.

It may or may not be an accident that in the trinity of thinking, feeling, and behaving, feeling is central. But I believe it says a lot that it forms the bridge between mind and body.

This active type of feeling may be intelligent but it shouldn't be mental; when it becomes mental, it turns into thought and has less contact with the body. Thought should not take over. You need to know how to think at your best, but you also need to disengage from it periodically. For instance, instead of anticipating (which is thinking that deals with the future) how an emotion will feel, it's better to just feel it in a fresh new way. Instead of getting lost in your approval/disapproval of the emotion, accept that it's there and feel it openly. Accepting an emotion doesn't mean you *agree* with it, but that you recognize it and its right to be.

Ultimately, what I am calling "feeling" is really love. Generosity and respect applied to your mind-body. This kind of love is not the romantic so much as the universal one (what the Greeks call *agapé*). The force and principle and fact that loves things, that wants them to be so they can be and are. It applies to all phenomena.

When you love something in this universal way, you allow it to live and prosper and do whatever it has to do. Regardless of this or that opinion. Applied to your own psychology, it entails allowing all your emotions—

whether positive or negative, so-called—to pulsate and course through your mind-body, and fulfill their purpose. Love is understanding things as they are, not necessarily as your personality wants them to be or thinks they should be.

Do you appreciate things? To *appreciate* something means you know its value. When a thing appreciates in value, it indicates more people are aware of its worth. Economics aside, do you find the "gold" in each thing? The medieval art of alchemy metaphorically described this process of finding the love and value that exists in things, hidden from ordinary consideration. Especially in yourself.

Feel to heal. Use your knowledge to support this endeavor. From inside, feel in your body while you do it.

With a new feeling experience, you may become conscious of something you weren't aware of before. "Pieces of the puzzle" that were hidden may come into plain view. The passive-reactive aspect's obstacles often lurk in the *semi-conscious* mind: though they manipulate, limit and coerce us, we're not really that familiar with them. We know something is wrong and that we could be better, but don't know what it is exactly or what to do about it precisely. When some situation sets us off and we react (get violent, shut down, tune out, get stiff, etc.), we're like a robot at that point and the passive-reactive aspect is holding the remote control. It has succeeded in

Concluding Remarks

sneaking up and taking over. So cultivating aware feeling fills a real and practical need, namely, changing your relationship to what your mind-body produces: in essence, becoming a conscious and understanding manager.

This book aims to help arouse that awareness which brings healing. Like all books, indeed like all words, it's a map of the way and not the way itself. Another book with a different or even contrary map may be just as valid. But if this book teaches you some things you didn't know and simplifies some things that were complicated, it's accomplishing something. A helpful map shows you a way and when you follow it, you move toward your destination.

Yet, each step along the way, as well as the rest stops and delays, is interesting and precious.

Suggested Reading

I have found the following books to be helpful and valuable. They are recommended for your consideration, though they may not necessarily be similar to the approaches featured in *Mind Managing*.

1. *Psychosynthesis* (Roberto Assagioli)
2. *Eight Lectures on Yoga* (Aleister Crowley)
3. *Doing Nothing* (Steven Harrison)
4. *Think On These Things* (Jiddhu Krishnamurti)
5. *Boundaries of the Soul* (June Singer)
6. *The Power of Now* (Eckhart Tolle)
7. *Tao Te Ching* (Lao Tsu)
8. *The Book: On the Taboo Against Knowing Who You Are* (Alan Watts)
9. *The Authorized Dark Zen Meditation Manual of Buddhism* (Zenmar)

About the Author

Alexander Chapunoff is a writer and licensed psycho therapist practicing in St. Petersburg, Florida. He has been a professional counselor for over sixteen years, and combines a particular form of client-centered rational-emotive-behavior therapy with solution-oriented Ericksonian counseling and mindfulness training.

www.ingramcontent.com/pod-product-compliance
Lightning Source LLC
LaVergne TN
LVHW011355080426
835511LV00005B/302